Let's Tell A Story

The Allegories of God

Sandra L. Ross

REJOICE
Essential Publishing

Dedication

"I will praise thee; for I am fearfully and wonderfully made marvelous are thy works; and that my soul knoweth right well."
— Psalms 139:14 KJV

Table of Contents

Acknowledgement

Thank you, Holy Spirit, for imparting and partnering with me to birth this book.

Introduction

It is so amazing how this book was inspired. It was just an ordinary day, and I was waiting in my car because it was too early to clock in for work. I began to feel the presence of God so strongly and I had an open vision. I saw this big wall and it was fortified. Then I saw and heard explosions like an air raid attack and the wall came down. The Lord told me, "Those walls are strongholds and like the Walls of Jericho, they will come down!" I also saw a big bridge and it was destroyed; it fell. I began to recite a childhood song, "*London Bridges falling down, falling down.*" I sang this song so many times as a child, but it was at that moment, God began to download to me so much revelation. The Holy Spirit began to minister and unveil the hidden gems of other childhood stories and nursery rhymes. The Lord instructed me to write "*The Allegories of God.*" It's a revelatory book that retells popular childhood stories and nursery rhymes with a creative twist by sharing the spiritual, and hidden treasures of wisdom, moral lessons, and encouragement in each story. I pray that you, the reader, that the eyes of your understanding be opened, and that God endows you with wisdom and revelation. Each chapter tells a story with the spiritual meaning and symbolism revealed to the reader. At the end of a chapter, there will be reflections that highlight the key points of the story and for the reader to ponder in greater depth. So, with all that said, "Are You Ready? and Are You Excited?"

CHAPTER ONE

Storyteller

Before I go any further, I feel led to lay the foundation of this book by giving you an understanding of the definition of a few words. *After all, Proverbs 3:5 says, "And with all thy getting get understanding."* According to OxfordLanguage.com, a story is defined as an account of imaginary or real people and events told for entertainment. Or an account of past events in someone's life or the evolution of something. In other words, a story can be called a narrative, tale, account, or history. So now you can see a storyteller is someone that tells stories. A few synonyms for storyteller are narrator, author, writer, and novelist. Telling stories is so significant, cultural, and historical. Whenever we would have family gatherings, the older folks would tell stories. I found these stories so fascinating because I would learn about my family history and gain a sense of who I am. Before there were books, stories would be told, and that person would be identified as the tribe, family or community historian, or oracle. These narratives would be passed on from generation to generation. My mother is called the walking, talking historian because she knows how everyone is connected by blood. She tells informative and exciting stories from her childhood and family life as a cotton picker and the Jim Crow era.

I remember when I was in the first grade and after doing our lessons, we would have story time. The teacher would sit on a small chair or stool and all of us kids would gather around in a circle. The teacher would either sing or recite a nursery rhyme or read from a book. She would use animated facial expressions, body antics, and different vocal sounds to keep us kids engaged. I had an aunt that could tell a story in a way that everyone would be in tears from laughing. She was a good storyteller. It is a proven fact that after an hour or two the listener is no longer listening to the speaker. Thus, the sign of an expert storyteller is someone that knows the following:

1. Knows their audience
2. Engages their audience by keeping their attention
3. Uses facial expressions, vocal tones, and is animated.
4. Discloses the intent of the story and its ending.

Jesus was an expert at telling stories and He would do so with parables. What are parables and why did Jesus speak in them? As stated in OxfordLanguage.com[1], parables are a simple story

1. Oxford Reference. 2022. parable. [online] Available at: <https://www.oxfordreference.com/view/10.1093/oi/authority.20110803100304891#:~:text=A%20simple%20story%20used%20to,side%20by%20side%2C%20application.> [Accessed 23 May 2022].

used to illustrate a moral or spiritual lesson, as told by Jesus in the Gospels. A parable isn't true nor is it historical. It's not a fairytale but is accurate to life itself. Parables use the imagination by using realistic situations. The Bible is full of parables. Examples are The Sower and The Good Samaritan. Jesus told stories that related to its time and often spoke about nature, farming, and plants. Thus, by using this approach, He was keeping the hearer's attention. Jesus spoke in parables to:

1. Captivate His audience.
2. Conceal the truth.
3. Make it relevant to the people.
4. To illustrate the truth in an illustrative way and prophecies.
5. The truth, to make it relevant to the people, to illustrate the truth and prophecies.
6. To help the hearers retain the meaning of the stories because it required the use of their imagination.
7. Reveal the hidden things of their hearts, dealt with sin, and hopefully caused one to repent.

Frankly speaking, when the Lord told me I would author a book called, *"The Allegories of God,"* I had no idea what an allegory really meant. I knew however that Hosea's marriage to a prostitute was symbolic of Israel serving other gods and that (Hosea 1-7) his life was an allegory. In my research, I learned that although a parable and an allegory are similar, they aren't the same. An allegory is defined as a story, poem, or picture that can be interpreted to reveal a hidden meaning, typically a moral or political one.[2] Dictionary.com defines it as a symbolic narrative.[3] In layperson terms, a parable is a short story that teaches a moral or spiritual lesson. An allegory is a work of art that reveals a hidden meaning, usually of moral importance. For fictional work, it often includes the usage of characters, settings, and or events that represent other issues.[4] Now that it is all clear, let us delve in on this fantastic adventure and let me tell you a story.

2. Oxford Reference. 2022. allegory. [online] Available at: <https://www.oxfordreference.com/view/10.1093/oi/authority.20110803095403338> [Accessed 23 May 2022].
3. www.dictionary.com. 2022. Definition of allegory | Dictionary.com. [online] Available at: <https://www.dictionary.com/browse/allegory> [Accessed 23 May 2022].
4. Writer's Digest. 2022. Uses of Allegory. [online] Available at: <https://www.writersdigest.com/improve-my-writing/uses-of-allegory#:~:text=An%20allegory%20is%20a%20narrative,The%20Pilgrim's%20Progress%20(1678).> [Accessed 23 May 2022].

CHAPTER TWO

Consistence Wins-
The Tortoise and the
Hare

"The race is not given to the swift or to the strong but to those that endure to the end."— Ecclesiastes 9:11 KJV

In *"The Tortoise and the Hare"* (Aesop), there's a race taking place with a crowd of different animal spectators from all over. The hare is the favorite and undisputed champion. The challenger comes forth and it's a tortoise and there's laughing. The hare looks at the tortoise and begins to laugh and mock him. The hare felt it would be an easy win and asked laughingly, "Why are you so slow?" The tortoise replies and says, "Let's race." One would ponder why would the tortoise challenge the hare? The tortoise knew and understood his strengths and weaknesses. The tortoise knew that although he was a slow creature, he had a robe on that read, **"True and Consistent."** *1 Samuel 16:7 says, "But the Lord said unto Samuel, look not on his countenance, or the height of his stature; because I have refused him: for the Lord seeth not as man seeth; for man looketh on the outward appearance, but the Lord looketh on the heart."* Samuel, a prophet of God, is instructed to go to Jesse in Bethlehem, for he has chosen one of his sons to be king. Samuel saw all seven of his sons and none were chosen as king. Samuel initially thought the firstborn was to be king because of how he looked and was corrected by God. Samuel inquired of Jesse if he had more children and Jesse told him, "My youngest but he's a shepherd boy," and Samuel asked him to bring him forward.

David, I'm sure didn't look like what Samuel imagined a future king would be. He was dirty and rough looking, but he had a superior quality about him. He had a beautiful countenance. Samuel anointed David as king. Jesse and his sons had dismissed David because they didn't even consider him by not including him. Have you ever been rejected because you don't look like the status quo? I can relate, and it doesn't feel good. I recall my Pastor at the time called me and told me that a fellow Pastor called him asking for a minister to bring forth the word at his church. I accepted and invited a sister who is a psalmist to go with me. When I arrived at the church and the Pastor saw I was a woman, he told me he didn't need me. Did this hurt? Of course it did. That night I brought forth the word at my church and God moved in a mighty way. Another time I was on a pulpit full of men and when I got up to speak, the men in the pulpit and some in the congregation stood up and turned their backs on me. I didn't get in my flesh, but I completed my assignment, and many were blessed. It's a sad situation when we count people out when, in fact, that person may have what you need spiritually.

The tortoise and the hare are at the starting line and the race begins. The hare takes off fast, sprinting and leaves the turtle in a cloud of dust. Everyone is laughing and picking at him because he's so slow. The hare feels he's so far ahead and decides to take a nap. The hare is a fast animal and because of this, he's arrogant and is confident in his own abilities. In high school, I tried out for the track team and I didn't make the cut. I lacked the speed and stamina as a sprinter. Later I realized, although not a sprinter, that I could run at a steady pace long distance. In the Navy I would run three to five miles every day because I knew my strength. The hare thought the race was only about speed, and boy was he wrong. The tortoise on the other hand, is a slow creature but he had enough confidence to challenge the hare to a race. He knew why he was created to be slow. A tortoise doesn't have to chase his food because he eats plants and they're stationary. The tortoise serves many benefits to the ecosystem and its eggs give nutrients to the sand on beaches. The tortoise sees the hare nowhere in sight, but he continues, slow and steady.

Ecclesiastes 9:11 reads, "The race is not given to the swift or to the strong but to the one that endures to the end." The tortoise had divine insight of this scripture, and that he was created on purpose for a purpose. His eyes were set on finishing his course.

Along the path to the finish line, he faced many afflictions and distractions, but he was relentless. He knew that he could do all things in Christ which strengthens him. The tortoise had a steadfast spirit and endured hardship like a good soldier in Jesus Christ. He used his shell as a hiding place from predators and storms at times. He didn't stay in his shell, the place of hiding and complacency. Nature was calling and he couldn't give up now.

Philippians 3:4 says, "I press towards the mark for the prize of the high calling of God in Christ Jesus." Press means to follow through (a course of action) and to push one's way.[5] The tortoise pressed and pushed past his circumstances. He didn't allow life to hinder him. He was focused and determined to continue for the mark of the prize. Several times in my walk in Christ, I wanted to quit and stay in a cave. A cave is where I just wanted to be just a pew member or seat warmer. I attended church and went home and all the while running from my calling because of church hurt. I did this for a while but I felt a press and a fire in my spirit. I kept hearing the Lord say, "It's not over till I say it's over." The hare failed to realize that the tortoise had a steadfast spirit and wasn't moved by the hardships he faced along the way. The hare's robe read, "**Quick Lighting**." The hare had speed, but he lacked stamina and focus. The hare realized he was ahead of the tortoise and got comfortable. He decided to sit down, and he fell asleep. The tortoise passed the hare and got close to the mark, the finish line. The hare woke up and lackadaisically sprinted to pass him. The story ends with the tortoise crossing the finish line first and being awarded the prize. The hare and

5.Merriam-Webster.com Dictionary, s.v. "press," accessed May 23, 2022, https://www.merriam-webster.com/dictionary/press.

the spectators were flabbergasted and wondered how did this happen? After all, the hare was a sure win. Speed out triumphs slowness any day, right? The hare lacked the staying power and tenacity which was his demise. He lacked the comprehension of who he was. Whereas the tortoise kept his eyes fixed on the task ahead and was determined to run the race and not be hindered. Consistency was the victor over speed.

REFLECTIONS:

1. Slow and steady wins the race. — Ecclesiastes 9:11

2. Be steadfast and unmovable in God. — 1 Corinthians 15:58

3. Don't put confidence in man or your own abilities. — Zechariah 4:6

4. When we set our eyes on Christ, we're able to serve Him better and finish the work. — Colossians 3:2, Matthew 6:33

5. It takes faith in knowing that God has put in you everything you need to be victorious and fulfill the assignment on your life. — Hebrews 12:1

6. The tortoise knew that in him resides greatness and the sky isn't the limit. He never gave up and he never quit. — Philippians 4:13

7. Never judge a book by the cover is an old cliché that's so true. Never underestimate or dismiss a person outwardly because God looks at the heart. — 1 Samuel 16:7

8. It takes wisdom, tough skin, and having a face like flint to handle the afflictions and storms that will surely come. — Ephesians 6:10

9. The tortoise was wise as a serpent and harmless as a dove. The tortoise didn't broadcast to alert the hare he was passing him. Don't tell your enemy your business. Be discreet. — Proverbs 2:11, Matthew 10:16

10. Don't allow opinions of man to dictate your day, peace, or joy. If the tortoise took in account when he was mocked for being slow, he wouldn't have finished the course. He knew the reason and how he was created, and this stayed with him. — Proverbs 29:25

11. God will silence your mockers and make you triumphant over your enemies. — Isaiah 54:17

12. The tortoise knew to use what was given to him in the time of danger. His shell was a hiding place. — Proverbs 18:10

13. The hare underestimated his opponent, lost his focus, and fell asleep. Stay woke. Be sober and watchful. Never sleep on the enemy. — 1 Peter 5:8

CHAPTER THREE

The Storms of Life-
Princess and the Pea

"To everything there is a season, and a time to every purpose under heaven." — Ecclesiastes 3:1

PRINCESS AND THE PEA

It is a customary thing or rule of thumb to avoid talking about the weather. It's deemed as taboo, especially when first meeting someone. However, it is my observation that asking, "How's the weather?" is because you want to know how to dress and is an ice breaker in social situations. Some care less about the weather because they feel they can't change it and it doesn't affect them. I do not concur with this. Weather is defined as[6]:

6. www.dictionary.com. 2022. Definition of weather | Dictionary.com. [online] Available at: <https://www.dictionary.com/browse/weather> [Accessed 23 May 2022].

1. **(noun)** The state of the atmosphere at a place and time regarding heat, dryness, sunshine, wind, rain, etc.
2. **(synonyms)** climate, temperature, humidity
3. **(verb)** Wear away and change the appearance or texture of (something) by prolonged exposure to the air.
4. **(synonyms)** weather-beaten, eroded, worn, unkempt, battered.
5. **Hebrew-** hold out, keep up, endure, stand, last out
6. **Greek-** survive

The location of a place determines the weather and seasons. Living in Alaska, its weather is not only different, but its seasons as well. The winter is 6 months of darkness and its summer is 6 months of daylight. The winds are extraordinarily strong that anything valuable you must chain down. It is often referred to the birthplace of earthquakes, so much so that the houses and buildings have wheels on them to move in unison during earthquakes. Moving to the east coast, there are four seasons. Living in NC, I quickly learned that there are seasonal hurricanes and tornadoes. Seasons are a measurement in time and their location has everything to do with it. Everything has a season and a purpose. So that tells us that storms have a purpose and before going any further, there needs to be an understanding of the word storm[7], which is significant to the story.

1. **(noun)** A violent disturbance of the atmosphere with fierce winds and usually rain, thunder, snow, or lightning.
2. **(synonyms)** uproar, commotion, trouble, disturbance.
3. **Greek-** Tempest, storm, rage, downfall.

7. www.dictionary.com. 2022. Definition of storm | Dictionary.com. [online] Available at: <https://www.dictionary.com/browse/storm> [Accessed 23 May 2022]

4. Hebrew- excitement, whirlwind, gust, upheaval.

Storms are seasonal, specific to certain locations and require certain elements of the weather to form. *Matthews 8:23-26 says, "And when he was entered into a ship, his disciples followed him. And behold, there arose a great tempest in the sea, insomuch that the ship was covered with the waves: but he was asleep. And his disciples came to him, and awoke Him, saying, Lord, save us: we perish. And he saith unto them, "Why are ye fearful, O ye of little faith?" Then he arose and rebuked the winds and the sea; then there was a great calm."*

The weather is not only affected by locations and seasons but certain elements create or form a storm.

Storm definition and meaning – Merriam-Webster[8]
1. A heavy fall of rain, snow, or sleet often with fierce winds.
2. To blow with violence.

Synonyms for storm:
Hurricane, tornado, typhoon, uproar, attack, assault, trouble, disturbance, downpour, blizzard, rough, turbulent, wild.

There was a prince that desired to marry a real princess and looked all over and could not find one. There were many counterfeits and there would always be something off and missing in them. After an extensive journey, the prince returned to his home unmarried. The prince needed to get adequate rest from his journey. Both King and Queen desired their son, the prince to be married. Unbeknown to them, their prayers were

8. Merriam-Webster.com Dictionary, s.v. "storm," accessed May 23, 2022, https://www.merriam-webster.com/dictionary/storm.

about to be answered. Everyone in the castle retired to their beds for the night. There was a heavy storm outside and late in the midnight hour there was knocking. The woman of the house, Mother Queen, went to answer the door. Wondering within herself, "What in the world? Who would be knocking at her door at this time of the night?" She opened the door and there was a woman that immediately stated, "I'm a Princess. I got lost in the storm." The woman was suspicious because looking at the stranger, she didn't look like a Princess. She was wet, muddy, and hair disheveled. The stranger looked like what she had been through. The Mother Queen couldn't get past her appearance and doubted she was being truthful. The woman was invited in, and her room was made ready. The servants were instructed to put twenty mattresses and twenty comforters on the bed. The Queen put a pea between the mattresses as a test. The next morning everyone was at the table eating breakfast and the Princess entered in. The Queen asked, "How did you sleep?" "I didn't sleep because I was so uncomfortable and I'm bruised all over," the princess replied. The Prince and the Queen knew that she was a real Princess, and the prince married her.

Psalms 139:14 reads, "I will praise You, for I am fearfully and wonderfully made; Marvelous are Your works, and that my souls know very well." One of the things that stands out is that, when the door opens, the Princess quickly identifies herself as a Princess. Secondly, she got lost in the storm. A Princess is a daughter of a King and a Queen, of noble blood, accustomed to the finer things in life, and lives a sheltered and pampered life. She finds herself walking around in a storm at night. Her carriage and guards are nowhere in sight. She's vulnerable. The Princess never had to work a day in her life. Climbing rough terrains, her hands touching things she never imagined she would. In spite all of that, she didn't allow her storm or affliction to change her identity. She knew who her father was, and she walked in that authority. The Princess didn't go out of her way to prove who she was, nor did she shout it from the rooftop. It was well within her soul that she was and is uniquely made and everything is good that dwells in her. She was anchored, safe in the fact that she was a Princess, and nothing could change that. She didn't allow her present situation to cancel or change her identity. Don't let your trails, afflictions, or storms dismiss who you are. The Lord will deliver you from them all. She said, "I'm a Princess," because she was anchored, confident in the fact, that she's the daughter of the King and had authority, power, and protection. It was embedded, imprinted in her that she was royalty, regardless of how she looked.

Paul, an apostle of Jesus and a prisoner, never forgot who he was. Paul was sitting by the fire and a viper bit his hand and he shook it off into the fire. Paul wasn't harmed nor was he worried because he knew who he was in Christ (Acts 28:3-6). The Princess was confirmed as being authentic because her skin was fragile and sensitive. She could discern that something wasn't right. Exhibiting that she would make a good leader and Queen because you must be sensitive and have compassion for your subjects. Have you ever experienced spiritual amnesia? It's when you're going through your season of trials and afflictions, you forget Jesus, the Word of God, your identity and power as a child of God. It's like a **"woe, it's me moment."**

There's so much in Matthew 8:23-26 because it's full of allegories and symbolism. Everything the disciples experienced, witnessed, and taught was intentional. It was a preparation for His earthly departure. Also, it is a narrative of what they would encounter and how to persevere in Him. In previous scriptures, Jesus tells the disciples to follow Him and that it won't be an easy or a comfortable commitment. Jesus entered a ship and the disciples followed Him. The sky is clear, and the sea waters are calm and the disciples are like, "Ok. It's just an ordinary day." They were fishermen, skilled, and felt confident in themselves. Out of nowhere, suddenly the skies turned dark, the wind was blowing hard, and the waves were bigger than they had ever experienced and overtakes the ship. The ship is being filled with water and is sinking fast. It looked like they were doomed and going to die. So, they go to the bottom of the ship, where Jesus is sleeping. They wake Jesus up in a panic saying, "Lord save us or we will perish." The disciples are rebuked, "Why are ye fearful, O ye of little faith?" Jesus arose and rebuked the winds and sea and there was a great calm. The disciples were full of astonishment that the winds and sea obeyed Him.

Our God is intentional and everything we may encounter has a purpose and a plan. Jesus was teaching the disciples that there's safety in Him and the power of knowing your authority. Jesus was able to speak to the storm and change took place because He knew who He was. In John 8:16, the soldiers came to arrest Jesus and told them, "I Am He," and they fell backward twice. Why? Because there's such an anointing, a power, and an authority in knowing who you are. Nothing will be impossible in Him. The sky is not the limit. It'll be, "I can do all things in

Christ which strengthen me." You will not waver but will be triumphant in whatever life brings you. Before his conversion Paul, an apostle of God, was a persecutor of the church and was relentless because he thought he was doing a worthy cause.

In Matthew 27, Apostle Paul and other prisoners enter a ship en route to Italy. Paul discerns a storm that would cause much damage, the loss of lives, and to change their course. The soldier believed the word of the master, then Paul. The south wind (the bringer of storms) blew softly, and they felt Paul was wrong. But not long after that, a storm arose and not just any kind of storm. It was a tempest Euroclydon storm, and the ship got caught in it. An Euroclydon is referred to as a Northeaster. It is a strong, rough, and freezing wind that blows from the northeast in the western and central Mediterranean, mostly in winter. A gregale can last four to five days. The sky was dark, and the ship was being tossed back and forth. They were taking a beating. They threw loads overboard to lighten the ship and even food. After a few days, we find Paul telling the people that they should have listened to him. But be encouraged. No life will be lost except the ship. After 14 days, four anchors were lowered, and many tried to jump ship. Paul tells them, "Stay in the boat and you will live but if you get out, you will surely die." They listened and arrived on land on broken pieces and not one was lost. Have you ever felt shipwrecked in your stormy season or so broken and felt you couldn't go on?

I remember asking God what's the purpose of storms in the natural and in the spiritual.

PHYSICAL STORMS.

1. Cleanse the air
2. Provides nutrients to the earth and growth takes place.
3. Replenishes the beaches, coastal area
4. Cleans the bacteria in the water

SPIRITUAL STORMS.

1. Matures us
2. Increases our faith
3. Transformation changes us for the better
4. Brings us closer to God
5. Births endurance
6. To position, reposition, or reset us.
7. Get our attention
8. To build us
9. For God to get the glory out of us.
10. To rely on God

In both passages, we see the importance of staying in the boat. Paul wasn't afraid but confident and was able to encourage others during a horrendous storm. Paul had weathered many storms and he learned that Jesus is an anchor. *Hebrews 6:19 says, "Which hope we have as an anchor of the soul, both sure and steadfast, which entereth into that within the veil."* The Princess didn't allow her present situation or the storm to rename her. You don't have to prove yourself to anyone nor shout from the roof top. God will confirm you; the anointing confirms that you are called and sent by God to do His work. The Princess was authenticated as real because the pea caused her to have an uncomfortable sleep and she was bruised badly. A true Princess' skin is fragile and overly sensitive and she has a compassionate heart. The Princess discerned that something wasn't right. She had all the qualities and makings of a good queen.

When the storms of life are raging and they surely will, it's so important to stay in the boat. Stay anchored. Even when the storm is at its worst, remember that greater is He that is in you than your present now. He's our shelter from the storm and a hiding place. Paul and everyone arrived in Malta (a place of honey and refuge) on broken pieces. The boat was ruined and damaged and the tattered pieces became a life raft for Jesus.

REFLECTIONS:

1. Trust and depend on God to navigate you, especially during the darkest hour. — Proverbs 3:5-6

2. Don't focus on your storm but let it be on God. — Colossians 3:2. Psalms 121, Jeremiah 29:13

3. Don't jump ship but stay in God and live. — John 15:4-8, James 4:8, Jeremiah 33:3

4. Don't judge but have compassion and empathy for others. — Matthew 7: 1-2, Ephesians 4:32, Matthew 7:5

5. Spiritual storms are seasonal, purposeful and for God to get the glory, to mature us and to bear fruit. — 1 Peter 5:1, 1 Peter 4:12-13

6. There is an anointing in knowing who you are in God. Thus the enemy is defeated. — Luke 10:19, Mark 16:18

CHAPTER FOUR

Toxic Entanglement-Dracula

"Be sober, be vigilant, because your adversary the devil walketh about as a roaring lion, seeking whom he may devour." — 1 Peter 5:8 KJV

I'll never forget I was in the eighth grade and one of my classmates was a bully. She had a lot of mouth and a big family. One day she wanted me to give her the answers to a test and I refused. Up to this point, we were okay because I helped her a few times, but she expected me to let her cheat off me all the time. So, she told me, "I'm going to get you after school." The majority of the class and school weren't fond of her but were too afraid to speak up. So, you know how it goes, the cowards wanted to see us fight. Long story made short, I didn't want to fight her, but she kept taunting me. Out of nowhere I ripped her shirt off her and went to town on her head. The fight didn't last long and was broken up because I was winning. I got suspended, but she never bothered me again. In fact, she and I spent time together a few times afterwards. Why did I tell you this? This bully was all mouth, and she had a lot of cohorts. The enemy is a pretender because he walks around like a lion, but he's not a lion. He is waiting and seeking an opportunity to gain access to prey upon you. Admittedly I was afraid but just like a New York rat, if you push it in a corner, it will attack you. My fear and being a man pleaser, gave her the right to use me (Proverbs 29:25). In other words, I allowed her to copy off me when I really didn't want to. My yay was a yay when I wanted it to be a nay and I became trapped in a position that I didn't like. When the enemy gains a legal right because of an open door, he gets angry and doesn't want to leave or let you go.

I recall a dream I had. I was in my bed sleeping and I heard my patio door in the living open. I could audibly hear someone walking in my house. I heard someone in my kitchen opening and closing cabinets loudly. I heard furniture being moved. In my spirit, I could hear my heart beating loudly and I knew I needed to see what was going on. So, in the spirit, I got up and walked into the kitchen and I saw this big dark figure stealing and taking my things. It acted like it had a right to be there. I rebuked the spirit, but it ignored me and continued in its actions. I heard the Holy Spirit say, *"No man enter into a strong man's house and spoil his goods, except he will first bind the strong man; and then he will spoil his house (Mark 3:27)."* The enemy had a legal right to plunder my things and bind me up. The Holy Ghost revealed to me that I needed to close doors that were open. I was legally separated from my ex, and I needed to confess anger and unforgiveness and repent. I asked Jesus to cleanse my heart and thus stripping the strongman of his goods and he had to go in Jesus' name.

Dracula, written by Bram Stoker, is a story that I enjoyed watching as a child, only later to regret it because I was afraid to go to sleep. Dracula is a folklore of a night creature that hungers for the blood of its prey. He is often portrayed as a handsome, distinguished, charming, and affluent gentleman. Looking outwardly and to an unsuspecting person, Dracula looked like he had it all together. But oh, looks can be deceiving. Case in point, Satan walks back and forth and roaring like a lion, seeking whom he may devour. So, Satan is a pretender and operates in deception and illusions. God doesn't look or is impressed by the outward man, but He discerns the inner, the heart of man. In the night, a horse and carriage arrived at Transylvania, the castle of Dracula. All that's unloaded is a coffin. People arrive at the castle for a visit, and it doesn't take long for the guests to notice that they only see him at night and never in the daytime. A rule of thumb that I practice is that if I enter a relationship or friendship and it causes me to deviate from God, then it's not wise to continue in it.

2 Corinthians 6:14 says, "Be not unequally yoked together with unbelievers: for what fellowship hath righteousness with unrighteousness? And what communion hath light with darkness?" In other words, and simply put, oil and water doesn't mix and neither does light and darkness. We are called to walk circumspectly and not as fools but to be cautious, watchful, and prudent be-cause the fallen world is full of evil, deceptions, and dangers (Ephesians 5:15-16).

I had a home with a well-manicured lawn and the landscape was beautiful with all kinds of flowers and plants. Sometimes people would get out of their cars and take pictures. But I had to be consistent when it came to my grass because no matter what, the weeds would always come back and try to destroy my lawn. The weed is invasive and chokes and takes nutrients from the grass. If not dealt with properly by killing the root, it will overtake your entire lawn. The enemy comes to steal, kill, and destroy. So, I had to be watchful and vigilant and consistent in killing them and in the end, I was the victor. However, the next season I couldn't get comfortable but be just as fervent. You can't afford to get comfortable with the enemy because he's not playing. If given an opportunity, he will devour you like a lion.

Dracula has a caretaker that tends to the safety of his coffin, and he does this because of the promise of being made immortal one day by his master. This is an example of a toxic relation-ship. I say this because Dracula needs the caretaker to watch over him and his coffin when he's sleeping and if he made him a creature of the night, Dracula would be vulnerable, so he's using him for his own agenda. The caretaker is an enabler, a person who encourages or makes it possible for another person to behave in a negative way to be self-destructive. For example, in Genesis 27:1-25, we see how Jacob and his mother were de-ceptive with Isaac in getting the blessing that was due to his oldest brother Esau. A toxic relationship is full of deception and entanglements. Everything isn't for us and it's so important that our desires agree with the father. I often pray, "Lord let my desires be your desires, and your plans be my plans. I submit my dreams, ministry, gifts, and talents unto you in Jesus' name (Psalms 37:4-5)." The caretaker's desire was not a God desire but a flesh desire. He wanted to live forever and be strong and powerful. All of which is full of selfishness. It's the carnal things that lead a man astray. Dracula meets the niece of one of his guests and immediately desires her because she reminds him of his bride that was killed centuries ago. Moving forward, Dracula enters her room every night to suck on her blood. He is sucking the life out of her. He's a spiritual leech, a vampire. The woman tries to resist him but can't because she's under a spell. She's now his victim. The niece becomes a creature of the night. At first, her cross keeps him away, but she lets her guard down by losing it. Thus, giving him access, an open window to feed on her.

I allowed sin to enter my heart and if Jesus had come at that moment, I would go to hell. The devil is very subtle and only needs an inch to gain a landing strip in our lives. Meanwhile, the caretaker, the enabler, becomes disgruntled because everyone is being changed and he's not. So, he leads the town people to the coffin of Dracula and in his anger, he bites and kills the caretaker for his betrayal. Dracula is killed along with his creatures. The niece lives and is changed back to her original state. The niece was loosed and set free, and the enemy was defeated. Proverbs 29:25 tells us that the fear of man bringeth a snare: but whoso putteth his trust in the Lord shall be safe. Fear of man, the need for approval and people pleasing always leads to compromising. The caretaker was afraid of his master, for he knew he was a monster. So provided him with victims by inviting them to the castle and made excuses for him during the day. If you were to yoke up oxen unequally, they would go in circles, or their efforts will be futile. The weaker oxen will be unable to keep up with the stronger oxen and the stronger oxen will eventually get tired or slow down to allow the weaker to catch up. The oxen lower its standards, and this is compromised in action. The caretaker tried to do the right thing in the end, but his seeds of corruption caught up with him.

REFLECTIONS:

1. The enemy is charming, cunning, and an opportunist. Seeking out its prey, looking for vulnerability and at the right time and undetected, bites the neck of its victim. We must always be on alert and prayerful so that we are not caught off guard by the enemy. — 1 Peter 5:8, Matthew 10:16, Psalms 144:1,

2. Don't be afraid of man that can only harm your body but fear God who is able to destroy our body and soul. — Matthew 10:28, 1 John 4:4, Romans 8:31

3. The caretaker wanted to be like a god. He wanted it all; to live forever and to be powerful. His heart wasn't right. He was dissatisfied with himself. He was insecure, and I would have to say the issues of the heart made him not value life. — Proverbs 4:23, Mark 8:36

4. Dracula's image and character were all a lie. His fruits were works of the flesh. The real him became known: a predator and perverted. What is hidden will always come

to light. — Luke 12: 2-3, Luke 8:17, Luke 12:3, Mark 4:22

5. Be careful who you allow access in your life and yield your ear to. You are judged by the company you keep and it can ruin your reputation and morals. — 1 Corinthians 15: 33, Proverbs 22:1, Ecclesiastes 7:11

6. When you're yoked up with the enemy, there's bondage and no peace. The vampires had an uncontrollable lust for blood and were tormented in their spirits. When Dracula was killed, the niece and others were set free and restored. Jesus' yoke is easy, liberating and there's rest and peace. — Matthew 11:28-30, Isaiah 10:27, John 8:3

CHAPTER FIVE

No Short Cuts– Three Little Pigs

"Therefore, whosoever heareth these sayings of mine, and doeth them, I will liken him unto a wise man, which build his house upon a rock:" — Matthew 7:24

The Three Little Pigs was originally written by James Halliwell-Phillips. It's a story that's been revamped and retold in different variations throughout the years. There was a mother pig and her three piglets that lived in a small house, inside the trunk of an oak tree. Mother instilled into them wisdom, excellent work ethics, and a solid foundation in God. She would often use the tree trunk as an example to teach them valuable lessons. Some of the lessons were Psalms 91:1-2, God is a refuge and a hiding place, and John 15:4-6, Stay in God because He's the true vine, the truth and we can't do anything without Him in our lives. The day came when the piglets were of age. Mother pig had poured into them like her parents did her. *Proverbs 22:6 says, "Train up a child in the way he should go: and when he is old, he will not depart from it."* She called them unto her and told them, "It's time for you to leave, go into the world, and live your life." Before their departure, she told them to never forget this piece of advice. "Whatever you do, make sure to do your best and that it'll save your life." Mother pig's heart was a little troubled, naturally as a mother would be. But she had an inward peace because she had raised them from piglets to pigs, boys to men in the admonition of the Lord.

Joshua 1:8 says, "This book of the law shall not depart out of thy mouth; but thou shall meditate therein day and night, that thou mayest observeth to do according to all that is written therein: for then thou shalt make thy way prosperous, and then thou shalt have good success." God was telling Joshua to never forget the law or Word and what he was taught; to keep it before him like frontlets. In doing so it will guide and keep him. Joshua meditated on the Word night and day. Praise God. So as a man thinketh so is he. The Word was hidden in his heart that he might not sin against God (Psalms 119:11). The Lord used Joshua to do great exploits and none of his enemies could stand before him. He walked in absolute obedience to the ordinances in God and everywhere the sole of his feet treaded upon was given to him, as promised to Moses. Joshua was bold and very courageous in the Lord and the words he spoke had authority because it was the Word.

The three pigs left and after a while, they found land that was to their liking. So, they decided to build a place to live. The youngest pig decided to make a house out of straw because it's the easiest and quickest to build in one day. The youngest pig wanted to play and do nothing. He was no longer under his mother's rules and chores. The oldest pig saw the house and warned the youngest pig that it doesn't look stable and that it won't protect them from the wolf. The youngest pig ignored his brother's warning and said, "Nothing is going to happen." The middle pig decided to build a house out of sticks and branches that he found in the forest. In three days, he built a small cubby hole and the oldest pig looked at it and told the middle pig, "Although you did a decent job building it, I don't think it's safe enough to protect us from the wolf." The middle pig told him, "Don't worry. It's safe," and dismissed his brother's warning. The middle and youngest pigs enjoyed their leisure. The oldest pig was taking his time in building his house. His house was made of brick and stone and took seven days to build. The other pigs looked at their brother and shook their hands and thought to themselves, "He's missing out on enjoying life." They continued to play, watch tv, and sleep.

One day a hungry wolf came looking for something to eat and he had a desire for ham and pork chops. He saw a house made of straw and the wolf banged on the door and told the youngest pig, "Open the door and let me in or I'll huff and puff and knock your house down." The youngest pig said, "Not by the hair of my chinny chin chin." A catchy phrase but that's all it was, for he knew he had cut corners in building his house. It was not his best effort. The wolf blew on the house, and it fell and blew away the straw in the wind. The youngest pig ran to the middle pig's house of sticks and branches. He was inside and the middle pig said, "Don't worry. We're safe." The wolf banged on the door and said, "Open the door and let me in or I'll huff and puff and blow your house down." The pig said, "Not by the hair of my chinny chin chin." Okay, here we go again, useless words that had no power. The pig knew he didn't build his house whole heartily. The wolf huffed and puffed twice, and the house fell. The pigs ran to the oldest pig's house, and they were let in. By this time, they were not only afraid, but their faith was at zero. The oldest brother pig said confidently and in authority because *Colossians 3:23-24 says, "Whatsoever ye do, do it heartily, as to the Lord, not as unto men; Knowing that of ye the Lord ye shall receive the reward of the inheritance: for ye serve the Lord Christ."*

He had built the best house he could build, and he knew it had a good foundation. He was sure because the lessons and wisdom his mother had imparted into him fell on good ground, his heart. He was a builder, and he knew that the fruit of his labor would be rewarded. The oldest pig reassured his brothers, "Don't fear. The wolf won't be able to destroy this house," and he locked the door with a deadbolt lock. The wolf banged on the door and the youngest and middle pigs were trembling in fear. You could hear their hearts beating fast. By this time, the wolf was angry, and the huffing made him hungrier. Just knowing that were three pigs to eat, he began to salivate more than ever. The wolf banged on the door loudly and with such force. "Let me in or I'll huff and puff and blow your house down." The oldest pig confidently said, "Do what you want, but you won't get in." The wolf huffed and puffed repeatedly with no success.

So, the wolf decided to enter in through the chimney. The pig quickly lit a fire and placed a pot of water on it. After a while, the wolf entered the chimney and fell into a pot of boiling water, and he was no more.

The next day the three pigs went to see their mother and the youngest pig said, "Mother you were right, that whatever you do, to always do your best." From that day forward, they were hardworking and lived a happy, safe life. Matthews 25:1-13 is a story about ten virgins. Five were foolish, forgetful, and so concerned about what was happening around them. They took their lamps with them to meet the bridegroom without extra oil. They were not prepared. The five wise virgins were attentive, detail-oriented and prepared because they took extra oil with them. The virgins got sleepy and fell asleep because there was a delay. It was nighttime and the groom arrived and the wise virgins prepared their lamps, and the foolish virgins had no oil in their lamps. They asked to borrow oil and was told no and went looking for oil to buy. The wise virgins were able to enter the wedding/feast and the doors were closed. The foolish virgins knocked on the door and was denied entrance. *Matthew 25:13 says, "Watch therefore, for ye know neither the day nor the hour wherein the Son of man cometh."* The foolish virgins were not ready because they were focused on the preparations of the day. They forgot to be prepared spiritually like Mary, whereas Martha was concerned about nonessential things that didn't edify her spirit.

REFLECTIONS:

1.   Everything we do in word or deed must be done in the Spirit of excellence. Excellent work ethics speak volumes and is a witness for Christ because it shows the light in you. — Colossians 3:23, Daniel 6:3, Proverbs 22:29.

2.   The oldest pig's arduous work paid off because he took no short cuts. He knew that his labor wasn't in vain and the work he did spoke for itself. He kept building while his brothers played and taunted him. — Galatians 6:9, Galatians 5:7, 1 Corinthians 15:58

3.   It's imperative that in doing the work of the Lord, there will be distractions, but they must not keep you from completing the work. Don't allow non-essential things to get you off course or to be not as mindful. — Matthew 6:33, Colossians 3:2, Proverbs 16:33

4.   Your foundation must be in God and His Word will keep, direct, and protect you. — Psalms 91:1-2, 1 Corinthians 16:13, Matthew 7:24

5.   Be ready for Christ's return, always, for it will come quick. Be found doing the work of the Lord and not slothful in the things of God. — Luke 19:33, Romans 12:11, and Philippians 2:12

6.   Don't allow people's opinions of you to hinder you. The fear of man will hinder the work of God in your life. It'll cause you to compromise or doubt what God told you to do. — Proverbs 29:25, Galatians 5:7, Psalms, and Philippians 3:14

CHAPTER SIX

No Vision- Rip Van Winkle

"Where there is no vision, the people perish: but he that keepeth the law, happy is he." — Proverbs 29:18

As a child, I would often hear, "An idle mind is the devil's playground or wake up before you sleep your life away." I remember my mother often saying this, especially on early Saturday mornings, to provoke my siblings and me to clean our rooms and do household chores. So naturally, I was intrigued when I heard about a man that slept his life away.

"Rip Van Winkle" (Washington Irving) is an interesting story that often left me wondering why, what, and how a person can sleep and miss life. In fact, a sad story that would motivate me

as a child to be industrious in my doings. Let's look at a couple of things before we go into the story. The name Rip Van Winkle means a person who sleeps a lot, a person who is oblivious to changes, especially in social attitudes or thoughts[9]. The word idle can be interpreted as a person avoiding work; lazy. Without purpose or effort; pointless. How fitting to the character and I'm a firm believer that it's important to be mindful what you name a child. Case in point, I worked as a correction nurse very briefly and I recollect processing in a young man, and I discerned such a darkness exuding from him. I asked him his name and he said, "Lucifer," and yes, that was his legal first name. He became his name and had committed horrendous monstrous acts. His name was his prophecy for his life.

Rip Van Winkle was a man without vision and purpose and because of that he was lazy. He had a great aversion to anything that required him to sweat or exert any physical strength. He became quite good at avoiding it by not being there through escapism.

He had a neglected farm that wasn't yielding any crop, the fences were torn, and his cattle roamed astray. He had two children, a son that resembled him so much and a daughter. Rip had no relation with his children because he was hardly there physically or emotionally. He also had a disgruntled, nagging wife. It was like he could never do anything right and dreaded being in his own home. *Proverbs 21:9 says, "It is better to dwell in the corner of the rooftop than with a brawling woman in a wide house."*

---

9. 2022. [online] Available at: <https://www.collinsdictionary.com/us/dictionary/english/rip-van-winkle#:~:text=Rip%20Van%20Winkle%20in%20British,Word%20origin> [Accessed 24 May 2022].

Granted and honestly speaking, Rip was very slack in his duties as a husband, father, and farmer. He was clueless and had no idea or plan to put his life in order. With his wife belittling him, I'm sure he felt more inadequate as a leader. *Proverbs 21:19 says, "It is better to dwell in the wilderness, than with a contentious and angry woman."* His wife was argumentative and incredibly angry and rightly so. She, however, didn't know her power as a woman and a wife. As a wife, she had inside of her the ability to speak words to buildup and draw out the greatness in Rip. She instead spoke death and not life. She was a foolish woman because she tore down her home vice building up her home like a virtuous woman. She would disrespect him on every occasion and in the presence of others (Proverbs 31). The townspeople would often haggle him because he was henpecked by his wife, and this brought him shame. *Proverbs 12:4 says, "A virtuous woman is a crown to her husband: but she maketh ashamed is as rottenness in his bones."*

In his home, he was a failure as a husband, father, and farmer. He found solace in the world, outside his home. Rip was a hero, a somebody. He was loved and seen as a kind man because he would play and make toys for the town kids. He was quick to help anyone in need. He was a frequent patron of the town's pub and there he was a man with a plan. He would tell hilarious jokes and outlandish tales and boy did he gossip. It didn't matter if it was true or not. Rip was empowered by destroying other reputations and lives because his was in such disarray (Proverbs 19:9).

Often as a way of escaping or running from his responsibilities, he would go to the Catskill Mountains. He took his dog Wolf and gun to go hunting, at least that's what he said, or they believed. Rip would talk and vent his cares to his dog for hours at a time. Saying stuff, he was too afraid to speak aloud. In the Bible, the wolf is depicted as wicked people, ferocious, treacherous, a predator, and a false prophet. Rip sought the comfort of a dog that couldn't help him instead of casting all his cares upon the Lord and making all his needs and supplications known unto God in prayer. The Catskills was a unique, beautiful, and enchanted place. He would sit for hours doing nothing. He was a do-nothing. Unbeknownst to him, today would not be an ordinary day. As he was walking, he saw a peculiar looking, short in stature man. The man was carrying a keg and he asked Rip to carry it for him and he did. The man offered him to take a drink and Rip did. It tasted like nothing he had ever tasted, and he began to drink it in excess. *Ephesians 5:18 says, "And be not drunk with wine, wherein in excess; but be filled with the spirit."*

Over the years with his frequent visits to the pub he acquired a liking for wine, and he used wine as a comforter. This only made things worse for him because it was another problem added to the equation. He was now a lazy drunk with no vision. So, when he tasted this wine, it was so good tasting, and he couldn't stop drinking it. He was hooked on the taste, and he had an uncontrollable lust for it. He didn't stop till he had consumed the entire keg. Rip wakes up and the first thing he says, "That was a long nap." Rip notices his beard is long and white, his gun is rusty, and his dog is nowhere in sight. He began to walk home and notices everything changed in town that his friends all have died. Rip inquires about his children and he's told they're alive, married and with children. He then hesitantly asks if his wife is alive, and he felt happy when he heard she died. He reconnects with is children and happily lives with his daughter. There's not much ado in Rip's life except being a good grandfather to his grandchildren and that's enough for him.

In Matthew 25:14-30, a man is going away on a journey and before leaving. He told his servants to take care of everything and he gave them each talents, and they all invested the talents and it increased in value. Except for one, he took the talent and hid it. The master returned and the servants were blessed for the increase in talents. The last servant told the master he didn't want to waste his money and so he hid it. The master rebuked him and called him a wicked and lazy servant. He allowed fear to stop him, and he didn't do anything. He was idle. *Romans 12:11 says, "Not slothful in business; fervent in serving the Lord."* God wants us to work, be industrious and not allow fear to stop us.

If Jesus allowed fear of man and death to stop him, there would be no remission of sin, no salvation or relationship. Jesus in three years went hard in the things of God and we are still affected by His ministry. Hiding the talent and not putting in any effort is the opposite of being steadfast, unstoppable, and fervent. The other servants stepped out on faith, took a risk and their efforts were rewarded. God rewards the work of our hands and makes them fruitful. The master was angry because he lived by the rule of sowing and reaping and lived off his increase. This servant neglected what he was given because he didn't want to do the labor that's required for the harvest to come. His slack caused the harvest to not be as plenteous as it could have been. So, the master not only rebuked him, but he also took his talent and gave it to the servant with ten talents and kicks him out of his house. The servant added no worth to his household, and he had poor work ethics.

REFLECTIONS:

1. It's important to have a vision for your life and to know your purpose. Without it, you'll lack guidance and direction in your life. — Hab.2:2-3, Proverbs 29:18
2. Walk in your God given authority, dominion, and power. — Genesis 1:26-28, Deuteronomy 28:13, Matthew 28:18
3. Be careful with who you share your inner most secrets because they can be a wolf in disguise. God will lead you to the right person in your time of need. — Psalms 1:1, Philippians 4:6-7, Proverbs 15:22
4. Rip lacked control with his appetite for wine, lying, and gossiping. He was filled with the things of the world instead of the things of God and the Word of God. — Proverbs 25:28, Ephesians 5:10
5. Too much rest and laziness will lead to poverty. Jesus worked in ministry and God rewards diligence. — Proverbs 19:15, 1 Timothy 5:8, 1 Corinthians 15:58
6. Be mindful of the words you speak because they carry weight in the spirit realm. You can cause damage with your words. Wars have started because of words and lies. Characters have been destroyed by rumors. We all will give account for every idle word we ever spoke. — Matthew 12:36, Proverbs 10:18, Proverbs 16:28

7. Rip and the servant were succumbed to fear, and they chose not to do anything. They preferred being idle. Fear will hold you captive and you will miss life. Fear cancels out faith and without faith, you won't please God. — 2 Timothy 1:7, Hebrews 11:6, Psalms 23:4

CHAPTER SEVEN

No Retreat- Little Miss Muffin

"Ye did run well; who did hinder you that ye not obey the truth?"
— Galatians 5:7

"Little Miss Muffin," is an English nursery rhyme by an unknown writer. Her real name is Patience and she's the step-
daughter of Dr. Moffett, an Entomologist (the study of insects).
Little Miss Muffin grew up in an environment with all kinds of
insects and creatures. Sometimes the critters would get out of
their containers and she and her father would play a game out
of who could catch them the quickest. Little Miss Muffin had
a love and fascination for bugs as well. Her father would often
share information from his research with her. As a daughter of
a renowned doctor, she was quite familiar and knowledgeable of

insects. Her friends were afraid to come to her house and even thought she was weird but to Little Miss Muffin it was her norm. On this day, Little Miss Muffin goes outside to eat and sits on a tiffin to eat a bowl of curds and whey. A tiffin is a small stool or chair, position and elevation and a bowl is a vessel for outpouring and receiving and the curd is the protein, nourishment of God's word. Her father made a little area just for her. It was beautiful and so relaxing. While eating, she sees a spider in her peripheral view that crawls near her. She drops her bowl and runs away, screaming like a wild alley cat. Poor Little Miss Muffin often would eat in this spot without incidence, but today, her norm had been rocked and she lost her bearings. Little Miss Muffin's father had poured into her countless hours, and she knew about every bug. Still, she allowed this spider to uproot her life and establish a position of unauthorized authority.

While Little Miss Muffin was in the house, the spider gained access to her tiffin. The spider spun a web on her tiffin and began to eat her food. Although she was taught well by her father and was quite knowledgeable, she was quick to run and drop everything, her life and crown (identity). She failed to stand because she abandoned or forgot the Word of God. Her fear and emotions caused her to have spiritual amnesia. That's exactly what the spider or the enemy wanted. So, it begins to spin a web on the tiffin and eats her bowl of curds. *Isaiah 7:9 says, "Stand firm in your faith or you'll fall for anything."* Little Miss Muffin had a giant in her life that was never dealt with. With her not standing, she compromised and gave the spider unlawful access. Her life, identity, purpose, power, and position were stolen, killed, and destroyed. Fear cancels and eradicates what God told has told you. Fear will take root in your life and take form if left untreated. The promises of God is squeezed out by the spirit of fear and its lies. Little Miss Muffin was overtaken by her emotions, runs into the house screaming. She knew her home was a place of safety. The name of the Lord is a strong tower and the righteous run to it and are safe (Proverbs 18:10). She sought the counsel of her father (Proverbs 11: 14) and told him everything that transpired. Her cares, fears, and supplications were made known. He didn't tell her to stay in the house, but he gave her another bowl of curds and whey.

He encouraged her and her faith was renewed, and she was strengthened by the power of his words (Ephesians 6:10). People of God, we may fall but the good news is we get right back up. Glory! Her father didn't tell Little Miss Muffin to stay in because he knew if she stayed in the house due to fear that she would never reach her full potential and but live a limited life. We know that Jesus came so that we could have an abundant life (John 10:10). Fear is a spirit that doesn't travel alone and will lead to other fears. For example, the fear of man and people pleasing. It'll cause you to compromise and be held captive later in life. Her father exhorted and prayed for her. He told her that it was time for her to face her giant. Mary was deathly afraid of spiders. Mary went back to her designated place and sat on her tiffin, thus putting her crown back on her head. She ate her bowl of curds, and it was good and from that time forward, she would do so, for she realized that greater was in her than any spider. She faced her giant; the spider and its power were destroyed in her life. She knew her purpose, position, and authority as a daughter of the doctor (Most High God). A little leaven destroys a whole loaf, and a little fear leads to more fear.

1 Samuel 17 tells the story of David and the giant Goliath. The children of Israel were in war with the Philistines. Goliath taunted and tormented them night and day. They had become weary and hopeless. They made the mistake of taking their eyes off God and focused on their present situation. In their fear, they forgot who they were and the God they served and His mighty acts. One day, David, a little shepherd boy and the youngest of Jesse's sons, was sent on an errand to bring food and check on his brothers. He hears the threats and teasing. He finds that Israel, the army of God, were afraid of Goliath. They got out of formation and fled for their lives out of fear. This mighty army got out of formation or position. They aborted and abandoned their identity and authority as the children of Israel. They acted like punks in the spirit rather than warriors of God. I can imagine when David saw this unfold before him, he was thinking to himself, "What in the world is going on here?" and "Oh, I know you didn't."

David was quick to address the enemy, Goliath, a Philistine, as less than and unclean. He knew the God he served, and His people were the army of God. He accepted the challenge to fight the giant. He was dressed in King Saul's armor, but he took it off because he had no battle history with it. It wasn't proven. So, David used what he was familiar with, a sling shot and five smooth stones he got from a brook. He was skillful with his weapons, and he had killed a bear and lion and he knew that the battle was the Lord's (1 Samuel 17:47). Surely the God of

Israel will be victorious, and he went forth with his staff, in the authority of God. He pursued, overtook, and overcame his enemy. He ran towards Goliath head on and face to face. David was questioned, teased, and dismissed by his brothers and now Goliath. David wasn't moved or doubted himself because he knew if God was for him, who could stand against him? He knew God was the strength of his life. Whom shall he fear and whom he shall be afraid of? There's a song, "I know who I am," and what a powerful song it is, and the enemy knows this as well. In fact, he dreads the day that you'll come into the knowledge and understanding of who you are as a child of God. He stands firm in a defensive stance and Goliath removes his helmet. He had sized up David and deemed it would be an easy win, a decision he would not live to regret. Goliath saw him as a child, but little did he know that God was with him and the God he served was mighty in battle. David took his sling and stone and shot Goliath in the center of his head, and he fell dead. Goliath had tormented and harassed the army of the living God with mind games. The Philistines had become their footstool.

REFLECTIONS:

1. Little Miss Muffin is young and respected, of prominent status. Little Miss Muffin was marked and separated because of her upbringing. Sometimes it can cause you to be seen as different and be by yourself. Little Miss Muffin didn't allow this to affect her. She was a happy child and well loved. We all may have distinct paths or lives. David was seen as a scruffy, little dirty shepherd boy who became king. Both Little Miss Muffin and David are often

seen as odd and unusual by people's standards. They were distinguished and chosen to be respected. They didn't succumb to fear by trying to fit in. When you embrace who, what and how you are in God, nothing will stop or limit you. — Psalms 139:14, 1 Peter 2:9, Proverbs 29:25, Romans 12:2

2. There must be no loose ends in our lives: issues that aren't dealt with, denied, or covered up. The fact of the matter, not talking about the issue doesn't make it disappear. The issue is still there and I've learned if you give the enemy an inch, he'll take a foot. It creates a landing strip in your life. Thus that gives him access and a first-class ticket. We see how fear can cause one to respond and be led by our emotions. Little Miss Muffin lost and forgot everything, and she retreated, only to face her giant like David did. When we face our giants and fears by standing firm on the Word of God, we are made victorious and our tormentors and harassers are silenced, having no power over us. — 2 Timothy 1:7, Isaiah 7:9, Ephesian 5:7

3. To accomplish and finish our mission requires a courageous heart, and we must be bold as lions. — Proverbs 28:1, Hebrews 4:17, Psalms 18:34

When seeking counsel, one must be careful who you seek out. The wrong and ungodly counsel can wreck and bring havoc to your life and be detrimental to your ambition and destiny. If Little Miss Muffin's father had told her to stay in the house, her outcome would have been different. Fear would have enslaved her. I've seen leaders and pastors suffering from depression, anxiety, and contemplating suicide. All because they didn't want to tell no one. Isolation and shame are a tactic of the enemy. Little Miss Muffin knew who to run to and where to go. She was safe and restored and faced her giant. — Proverbs 11:14, Proverbs 15:22, Psalms 46:1, Psalms 32:7, Psalms 4:8, Psalms 9:9

5.   Whatever you do, don't run and abandon your crown and position. The enemy is a pretender and perpetrator and he uses mirages and illusions to deceive and hinder God's people. Remember who your father is and say, "It's just an illusion." "Imagination," a song that I loved as a teenager, is about looking for a destiny, a picture, or something that's not real and causes your emotions to be all over the place and to be confused. Open your eyes and look around. It's just an illusion and all this confusion. When you realize it, you'll be free and have peace. — 1 Peter 5:8, 2 Corinthians 10:5, James 4:7, Ephesians 6:11

CHAPTER EIGHT

A Change of Heart-
Beauty and the Beast

"A new heart also will I give you, and a new spirit will I put within you: and I will give you a heart of flesh." — *Ezekiel 36:26*

Have you ever met a person and just by looking at them, you can tell that they had a hard life and been through a lot? Or you met a person, and they told you how old they are, and you are surprised because they look much older. I met and worked with such a person. I was 18 years old and working in a factory. There was this woman I'll call Ruth and for the life of me, I couldn't understand why she didn't like me. This woman would get in my face and call me a Yellow "B---H." I wasn't saved but It didn't take a rocket scientist that she was full of anger and very bitter. She had few teeth in her mouth and the few she had were rotten and she had long dark nails full of dirt. She had suffered things in life, a drug addiction, jail, and domestic abuse. I told my mother what was going on and that I didn't want to disrespect her because she was my elder. It's crazy but I felt sorry for her. My mother said, "You're grown and the next time she gets in your face, curse her out." Ruth cursed me out the next day and I told her that I would give her a beat down after work. Well let's say Ruth left work early that day and she never bothered me again. I told you about her because pain and tough times changed her and caused her to deflect on others.

"Beauty and the Beast," is a 18th century fairytale, originally written by Gabrielle- Suzanne de Barbote Villeneuve. It's a story of a young prince that was cursed and turned into a beast. The beast has lived in his present state for 7 years. Rumor has it that the prince was very selfish and treated people cruelly. He thought highly of himself and saw others as beneath him. *Philippians 2:3 says, "Let nothing be done through strife or vainglory; but in lowliness of mind let each esteem other better than themselves."* For this reason, when he was eleven years of age, he was cursed by a stranger, a witch, whom he had treated badly. She told the young prince that the curse would be broken when he learns to treat others kindly. He tried to have the curse reversed to no avail. The beast lived an isolated and miserable life in his castle. Everything connected or attached to him was dead, dark, and dreary. The castle was dark, and the landscapes and gardens were also dead except for a lone, beautiful red rose. It was like he was a dark cloud and if anyone came near his castle or property, he would chase and scare them away. Because he was full of anger, he would have fits of uncontrollable rage. At night

he takes off his clothes, runs wild, roars, and howls like a crazed animal. The townspeople were afraid of him, and the children would sneak and throw rocks at his windows. He pushed everyone out of his life. His parents were dead and all his servants were scared or dead. The beast had no friends or visitors, for he didn't know how to have and form relationships. He felt people couldn't see past his outer appearance and his behavior didn't make it easy.

Sometimes the curve balls a person may experience in life will mar and hinder their ability to establish healthy ones. I know for me, I lived in self-preservation mode because of abuse. I was full of mistrust and hated anyone trying to get close to me. But in God and His love, I was able to open and have friendships. *"A man that hath friends must shew himself friendly: and there is a friend that sticketh closer than a brother (Proverbs 18:24)."* One day a young girl name Beauty is out walking and enjoying the scenery when she notices a castle in the distance. She lived a sheltered life and wandered off farther than she was supposed to. She sees a garden and everything is dead except a beautiful red rose. Beauty picks the rose for herself. It started to rain and she decided to go into the castle until the storm passed. Upon entering, she cries out, "Hello, is anyone here?" but no one answers." She's walking around the castle looking and touching things. Everything is so dusty. Beauty decides to take a nap until the rain stops and she wakes up to find a table full of fine foods and delicacies. The Beast enters the room and Beauty is startled by his appearance and she hides her fear with a small smile. There is small conversation and Beast only talks about himself. She thinks to herself how conceited he is and never once tried to engage her in conversation. Beauty had the beautiful rose she had previously picked on her lap and she showed it to him. The Beast yells at her and calls her an imbecile and that what she did was punishable by death, and he tells her that he will harm her entire family. Beauty flees from the castle and she runs to tell her father and her brothers were so angry.

The next day the father meets with the Beast, and he tells him, "I will spare your family in exchange for Beauty to live in my castle as my fiancée." They agree and he asks that Beauty doesn't know the full details of the agreement. Upon returning home, her father tells her of the agreement as he couldn't lie to his daughter, Beauty. The next day she goes back, and she speaks the truth in love to him, that his behavior is unacceptable and outright rude. The Beast never had anyone speak to him in such a bold way. He gets in her face, yells and tries to scare her but she's not afraid. She realizes that he does that to keep people away. Beauty holds the Beast accountable for his negative behavior and she counteracts it with words of encouragement and she's patient with him. She discerns a greater issue and that something has made him the way he was, and she wanted to know why and if it was possible to help him. No one knows this but the Beast has prayed for help. He wanted to love but he didn't know how, and he didn't want to be so angry.

Beauty knew something happened to him to cause him to be a Beast and to suffer alone in misery. Beauty shows up and her compassion was resilient, and it began to chip away at his hard heart. His heart was unlocked and everything in him changed. His life became colorful. His gardens bloomed. The castle's drapes on the windows were removed to let the sunlight in and his servants were quickened and made alive. There was jubilee and celebration taking place. The Beast gave love another try and they were married. He came into covenant with Beauty. With love and kindness, God draws all men.

Daniel 4 talks about Nebuchadnezzar, who was a popular king that was skilled in battle. He had a big flourishing kingdom and a superior army that won many battles. He was a man full of pride and he felt he and his kingdom were the greatest. He refused to acknowledge God and to give Him the glory due to His name. Every knee shall bow, and every tongue shall confess that He is Lord. Because of Nebuchadnezzar's pride, he was turned into a beast. He became like a lunatic and crawled on all fours like a wild beast. His nails grew like claws, and he ate grass like an animal, and growled like one. He was in this state for 7 years. The next time he spoke, he gave God the glory and his mind and kingdom were restored. Nebuchadnezzar was humbled and he was never the same again and for the good. Beauty symbolizes the perfect love of God in 1 Corinthians 13. Love is patient and kind. It doesn't judge or condemn but it restores. If your brother is overtaken in a fault, those of you who are spiritual restore them in love. God is faithful. Great is thy faithfulness. He will never leave or forsake you. God desires that none would perish but all come into repentance.

The beast is symbolic of the flesh, a hard heart and what pain can do to a person; its anger, rage, and unforgiveness. King Nebuchadnezzar is the lust of the flesh, the lust of the eyes and the pride of life. The warning comes first before the fall. In

Exodus 35, Moses asked the people for a free will offering of the heart. You must be willing to surrender and humble yourself under the mighty hand of God. God told Jeremiah, "I will restore you and I will rebuild you." A man's ways may seem right to him, but it takes the Lord to reveal it to him, so that he gets it right (Proverbs 21:2). The pure in heart shall see God and the meek shall inherit the earth. The beast was a byproduct of what happened to him, and Nebuchadnezzar was arrogant. He sinned and had to reap the wages of sin. Acknowledgement, confession, and repentance is the pathway to healing and restoration. Lean not to thy own understanding but in all thy ways acknowledge him and God shall direct thy path. Both lives and situations were changed. They were never the same. Old patterns were broken. Strongholds were destroyed and burdens were lifted. Yokes were removed and destroyed. They were given a new heart, right spirit and a new mindset: the mind of Christ.

REFLECTIONS:

1. The Beast is a young prince who lived a privileged and spoiled life. His behavior was never corrected because of who he was, a prince. So much so that he was turned into a beast, which is symbolic of what was in his heart. God desires that none would perish but come to repentance. He will chasten us because He loves us so much. After seven years, He sent him his destiny helper and after a while, the Love of the Father wins and his heart is changed to flesh. Beauty, which is symbolic of the Love of God, didn't judge. She was patient, kind, and unjudgmental. — 1

Corinthians 13:4-8, Jeremiah 31:3, 1 Peter 4:7, Proverbs 15:1

2. Most of the battles are in our minds and we need to come out of agreement with the enemy. Old thoughts will be annihilated with a sanctified and disciplined mind. When the enemy tells us things contrary to God's Word concerning us, be quick to bring those thoughts unto the obedience of Christ. Or when he mentions your past, tell him, "Satan, that's the past and God is doing a new thing in me. I see it and I walk in it in Jesus' name." — 2 Corinthians 5:17, Isaiah 43:19, Philippians 4:8, Romans 12:2

3. The love of Christ is an agape love that's powerful. If we don't love, we're not of Him because God is love. Love broke the Beast and the King out of slavery. Although different approaches were used, the Father chastens those He loves and its love that wins. — Hebrews 12:6, John 13:34-35, 1 John 4:7-8, Galatians 6:1

4. Nothing is too hard for God; no job is too small or too big. He is bigger than any situation, issue, hurt, pride, and more. The Beast lost all but your hope must be anchored in Jesus even when you feel it's a long journey. God made and He knows the heart. Only He can change it. Ask Esther. — 1 Corinthians 2:11, Proverbs 21:1, Psalms 139:23-24

5. Often humility and meekness are looked at as a sign of weakness. Oh so not true. Jesus could have called on a legion of angels, but He didn't. Both the Beast and Nebuchadnezzar had to be humbled due to the issues of pride and other things. The flesh had to submit to the

authority of God and His love dealt with heart's issues.
Once completed, after seven years, they were restored. I
remember for a season after the Navy I went through a
time of living poor. I had shoes with holes and used boxed
perms and church folks made fun of me. After graduat-
ing from nursing school that all changed. I shopped till
I dropped, traveled and with that came pride and arro-
gance. The truth was spoken to me in love by my pastors.
I received and acknowledged it as true. Once I repented
and had Godly sorrow, I was restored and learned to not
love the blessing more than the Blesser. I was always a
giver, but I gave even more. Glory!!! Afterward the Beast
and the King were never the same. God was given His
glory and people were treated with kindness and compassion. God makes all things beautiful in His time. All things
work together for the good! — James 4:10, Colossians
3:12, Proverbs 22:4, Proverbs 15:33, and Romans 8:28

CHAPTER NINE

Listen and Obey-Little Red Riding Hood

"But Samuel said, Hath the Lord as great delight in burnt offerings and sacrifices, as in obeying the voice of the Lord? Behold, to obey is better than sacrifice, and to hearken than the fat of rams." —1 Samuel 15:22

"*Little Red Riding Hood*" originally written by Charles Perrault, is a fairy tale of a young country girl who wore a red cape everywhere she went. Therefore, everyone called her Red. It had been a while since she last visited her grandma and she asked her mom if she could see her. Her mother said, "Yes, that's a clever idea but first, let me pack a basket to give to her." Before leaving, her mother looks at her intensely and tells her to hurry along and don't be idle. Remember what I taught you, "Don't speak to strangers." Following the familiar path that leads to her grandma's, Red sees beautiful flowers and butterflies. She decides I'll take one to grandma, but there are so many and each more beautiful than the another. She begins to pick flower after flower and is so encamped that she doesn't pay attention to the time. Little does Red know that she's being watched by a dark shadow behind a tree, waiting for an opportunity.

1 Peter 5:8 tells us, "Be sober, be vigilant; because your adversary the devil, as a roaring lion, walketh about, seeking whom he may devour." The wolf appears and he speaks in a soft and friendly tone with all his might. He asks her why she's in the deep part of the forest all alone. Red is taken off guard by his friendly demeanor and begins to engage in a conversation with the wolf. She tells him everything and even points to the direction of her grandma's cottage. After a while, she says to the wolf, "It was nice meeting you, but I must go," and she continues her path. The wolf takes a shortcut and arrives at the cottage before Red. He taps on the door lightly and grandma thinking its Red says, "Come in. I was wondering if you were coming at all." The wolf eats the grandma before she could respond. The wolf puts on a robe and bonnet from her closet and a dab of her perfume behind his ears. He barely gets in bed before there's a knock on the door. Red enters and immediately feels something isn't right, but she couldn't put her finger on it. She asked her grandma, "Why are you in bed?" The wolf said, "I was taking a nap." Red said, "Oh grandma why does your voice sound raspy?" and the wolf said,

"I have a cold." Red rubs her head and asks, "Oh grandma what big ears you have?" The wolf says, "To hear you better." Red said, "Oh what big eyes you have." The wolf says, "To see you better." Red gets closer to the bed and says, "Oh what big teeth you have," and the wolf says, "To eat you all the better."

The wolf chases Red around the cabin and Red runs out the door screaming, "Help! Help! There's a Big Bad Wolf trying to eat me!" A hunter was nearby, and he came running and he caught the wolf and made him cough up the grandma and he took the wolf to the deepest part of the forest where he couldn't harm another. Red and her grandma sit down, eat lunch, and discuss the importance of obedience. There are different endings told by various writers. In one version, the hunter kills the wolf and cuts open his stomach, pulls out the grandma, and she lives. In another version, the wolf eats both Red Riding Hood and her grandma in the end. In 1 Samuel 15:1-23, King Saul is given specific instructions by God regarding the Philistines. He responds with partial obedience because he doesn't want the people to be mad at him and then offers up an offering to God. The fear of man is a snare, but whoever trusts in the Lord is kept safe. Partial obedience is disobedience to God and King Saul is rejected by God and He snatches the kingdom from Him.

In 1 Kings 13:11-25, a young prophet is given clear and precise instructions by God to not eat or drink anything and not return the way he came. He believed the word of the old prophet rather than the commandment of God. The young prophet lost his life in the end, for the wages of sin is death. It can be spiritual and physical, and he lost his physical life. We see in each

scenario instructions are given for each task. Obedience is critical and discernment is necessary. The red hood is symbolic of
a covering. It provides safety and covers sin. Red is symbolic of
warfare, death, and sin. The wolf is symbolic of a stranger, ferocious, the enemy and a predator. The forest is symbolic of the
world. The mother knew Red following her commands would
keep her safe. The Word of God is the bread of life and if we love
Him, we will keep His commandments.

REFLECTIONS:

1. As God's people, we live in the world, but we are not of
   the world. The Blood of Jesus covers us, and we are made
   safe because He's our strong tower. The Word of God is
   the bread of life, and we see how Jesus was tempted by the
   enemy in the desert. A place of testing and the only thing
   He relied upon was the Word itself and He defeated the
   enemy. Thy Word is a lamp unto my feet and a light unto
   thy path. Jesus sent the disciples out two by two and gave
   them instructions. They were sent with the word that He
   imparted into them. The young prophet was found sitting under a tree. He was covered as long as he adhered to
   the commandments. Once he disobeyed, he was no longer
   protected. The Red hood was a covering and as long as
   she stayed on the right course, she was safe and secure.
   The Word of God is sound counsel and in the multitude
   of counsel, there is safety.

2. You must understand the assignment for your life and
   how it affects others. Our sin will affect generations to
   come. We see David's lust issues visited upon the next

generation. Tamar, his daughter, was raped by Amnon, her brother. David's other son, Solomon also had lustful problems. Red Riding Hood cost her grandma being eaten, and the young prophet lost his life. Think about the things and people's lives he could have impacted had he obeyed God. Saul's kingdom was ripped from his hands because he more concerned with pleasing man than God. One must have a, "for God I live and for God, I'll die." Anything less will stop the work; it will hinder you from finishing your course. There is much to learn from this narrative. Pray for wisdom and discretion. Don't tell everything to everybody. Pray for discernment because your enemy will use your secrets to destroy you. The wolf pretended to be nice, but he was a wolf in sheep's clothing. I can't tell you countless times I cried because a leader disclosed info to other church folk. Just because he or she has a title doesn't mean they can hold water. I use wisdom and discernment in who I share confidential matters. I have a covenant sister and it's an ordained David and Johnathan relationship. — 2 Corinthians 2:11, Proverbs 2:11, Ephesians 1:18, Matthew 10:16, 1 Thessalonians 5:12, Matthew 5:37, Luke 11:28, Deut. 5:33, Prov. 10:17, Joshua 1:8, Romans 8:4, Psalms 128:1

CHAPTER TEN

Stay Focused- Little Bo Beep

"But seek ye first the kingdom of God, and his righteousness; and all these things shall be added unto you." — *Matthew 6:33*

"Little Bo Peep," is a nursery rhyme originally written by James William Elliot. Mother Goose rewrote a more popular version. Little Bo Peep is a young sheep herder that was given her name by a seasoned shepherd. It's similar to the sound sheep make, "Bleat, Bleat." Tending to sheep is no easy matter. You are responsible for everything that pertains to them. She led them to the best grass, tended to their wounds, and treated their coats of wool with special treatments. She endured the harsh environments and never really got sound sleep because she was

always watching out for the enemy. Little Bo Peep knew a shepherd's life wasn't easy but it was far rougher than she imagined.

The long days and nights with the little sleep took their toll on her. On this day, she led the sheep to a beautiful valley with the most succulent grass. The sheep ate and were full and on their way to sleep, Little Bo Peep settled down with the sheep whom she loved and had even named them according to their own quirky temperament. She was playing soft music from her flute and before no time, they were all sleeping. Little Bo Peep counted the sheep one by one, and she fell asleep in the process. Poor Little Bo Peep, when she woke up she realized her sheep were missing. Little Bo Peep looked everywhere. She asked everyone, "Have you seen my sheep?" They told her, "Don't worry. They'll come back eventually." This wasn't comforting at all, but she cried more than ever. She was heartbroken because her one job was to care for the sheep, but she got comfortable and distracted by the beauty of her surroundings. Truthfully speaking, Little Bo Peep said within herself I'm going to close my eyes just for a second and it was the reason she lost her sheep, wealth, and livelihood. Some interpretations say she lost one sheep while others don't disclose the exact amount. In any case, it didn't matter if it was one or several because she valued each sheep's life. She was frightful because the longer the sheep was lost, the greater its chance of being eaten by wolves.

Just sitting around and hoping her sheep would come back wasn't enough for her. She decided to keep looking and when she was in the direction of her home and as she went over the hill, she heard the happiest sound ever, "Bleat! Bleat!" Her scattered sheep ran towards her. They were safe, but they were missing their tails. Little Bo Beep didn't want to think or fathom what the sheep may have encountered. Little Bo Peep was thrilled they were all safe. She would bandage their broken tails and in no time, all will be restored.

The Parable of the Lost Coin in Luke 15:8-10 tells of a poor woman who lost a coin. It's possible it was the wages she earned from hard labor, and her entire life savings. A savings she believed for a better life and or for emergency funds. When the woman lost her coins, there's such an urgency in her because it was all she had. She needed to buy food and other things. She swept her entire house nonstop and lit a candle under the table, bed, and every dark place. After some time, she finds her lost coin and rejoices because all hope has been restored. What was lost is now found and she told her neighbors and they rejoiced with her. Rejoice with those who rejoice and weep with those who weep (Romans 12:15).

Matthew 18:10-14 is another great parable of a shepherd leaving behind his ninety-nine sheep to find one sheep. When the one lost sheep is found, he rejoices more over the one than the ninety-nine he had. In each story, the sheep and the coin represent a human that has strayed away or got off course from God. It is the story of being lost, being found, and restored. The loss of one soul matters to God. **"All Souls, All Lives Matter to God."** *Luke 15:7 says, "I say unto you that likewise more joy shall be in Heaven over one sinner that repenteth, than over the ninety nine just persons who need no repentance."* Little Bo Peep learned a hard but valuable lesson that to whom much is given, much is required. Unfortunately, many Pastors have lost their passion and love for the sheep. Many are wolves in sheep's clothing and care more about building a golden calve: Big buildings, pockets fat from fleecing God's people, and promoting their name vice the name of Jesus Christ.

REFLECTIONS:

1. When doing the work of God, there will be times you may be weary. Little Bo Peep became weary when she focused on the harshness of her job. She listened to her flesh and compromised, which birthed negligence. — Philippians 3:14, Colossians 3:2, Matthew 6:33.

2. A good shepherd tends to the sheep and doesn't scatter them. He loves the sheep and the sheep loves Him with the pure Word of God. — Matthew 25:23 Jeremiah 23:1, Luke 12:48, 2 Peter 1:19.

3. Your actions not only affect you but what and who is connected to you. We must not be slothful in the things of God. Little Bo Peep reaped what she sowed and what was manifested was losing her sheep. But in her not listening to people, she acted by looking all over for her sheep. Whereas the poor woman's efforts in looking for her lost coin and lost sheep was found and there was rejoicing. — Jeremiah 29:13, Galatians 6:7-9, Proverbs 14:23-33, Luke 15:32

4. Excellent work ethics and behaviors represent the Christ in you. You will do the right thing all the time, even when no one is watching because you know God sees. Integrity

will keep you from making bad decisions. — Proverbs 10:9, Mark 14:38, Matthew 26:41

CHAPTER ELEVEN

A Great Fall-
Humpty Dumpty

"*Some trust in chariots, and some trust in horses: but we will re-member the name of the Lord our God.*" — *Psalms 20:7*

"*Humpty Dumpty*" written by Mother Goose, is one of my favorite nursery rhymes. There is so much symbolism in this rhyme. The name Humpty Dumpty in the 17th century referred to a brandy type drink. It also was a slang name for a short and clumsy person. In my research, I discovered two back stories to this rhyme. King Richard 3rd had a horse name Wall and in battle, he fell off his horse. He was bludgeoned in the head, and they couldn't restore him. Another version depicts it's about a king whose wall was destroyed by a cannon named Humpty Dumpty. The king's men tried and were unable to restore him to his rightful regal position. Ok so that's the end of a brief history lesson.

Merriam- Webster dictionary defines an egg as a hard-shelled reproductive body produced by a bird and especially by the common domestic chicken. Also, its contents are used for food. It's an animal's reproductive body consisting of an ovum together with its nutritive and protective envelopes and having the capacity to develop into a new individual capable of independent existence. An egg's exterior is quite fragile. However, if you were to put an egg in the palm of your hand and squeeze, the egg won't break. Wall is defined as a continuous vertical brick or stone structure that encloses or divides an area of land; enclose (an area) within walls, especially to protect it or lend it some privacy. The synonyms for a wall are barricade, barrier, partition, fortification, and separator. Some purposes of a wall are to support rooves, ceilings, and floors.[10]

Humpty Dumpty was an egg of prestige. He was well dressed and sat high upon a wall. A wall that was positioned in such a way that people would see him in their coming in and their going out. There was no way he could ever be overlooked. The wall, which was thick and fortified, provided him safety. Humpty Dumpty took pride in his place of position on the wall. He felt powerful and unconquerable. There was one major issue. He was an egg. One day Humpty fell off the wall and landed on the ground, his shell cracked, and all his inwards were exposed and spilled out. All the men that tended to and served him couldn't, no matter how hard they tried to put him back together again. Humpty

10. Merriam-Webster.com Dictionary, s.v. "egg," accessed May 24, 2022, https://www.merriam-webster.com/dictionary/egg.

was broken in so many pieces. He was just an egg. Have you ever met someone who, by looking at them on the outside, appears they got it going on or all together? We have a lot of that in the house of God and I call them pretenders. I say this because I was one of them. I worked hard to hide my pain by never being seen without a full face of makeup. My hair was done every week and I shopped at the most expensive boutiques. Someone would ask, "What's wrong with that?" Nothing is wrong with looking your best, but it was a coverup of what was going on in the inside. I was pretty and dying at the same time. You'll be surprised how many saints sitting on the pews in all their glam are crying on the inside. Humpty Dumpty looked confident but he was insecure and made his wall his security blanket. He was full of pride. He had everything: position, prestige, and people that were at his disposal. He was seated above people, and he was seen and esteemed by the people. There's a question one must ponder. Why or what made Humpty Dumpty fall? Wow! What a loaded question and one that I will gladly answer by way of an explanation.

In ancient times, potters would make vases which were especially important. After a vase is made, the potter would hold up the vase towards the sunlight and if a crack were seen, it was deemed defective, and the potter would break it and start the process all over again. This may sound extreme, but a vase is a vessel created to contain and a crack would lead to leaks. Think about this, in Jeremiah 18:1-5, the Potter is God, and the clay is God's people. The more pliable and yielded the clay, the easier it is to mold and shape. Thus, creating the best vessel to contain what it was created to do or hold. The wheel depicts transformation and process. We must keep a yes in our spirit and allow him to have his own way with us. Molding and shaping us, never thinking we don't need Him anymore or thinking we've have arrived. *Philippians 1:6 says, "Being confident of this, that He who has begun a good work in you will carry it on to completion until that day of Christ Jesus."* A song I recall the kids would sing, "Please be patient with me. God is not through with me yet."

Earlier in defining an egg, we noted that the inside of an egg is to be eaten. If an egg is fertilized, it will live off the nutritional substance inside the shell and while viable, would break out of its shell and live an independent existence. Humpty Dumpty was an egg that wasn't living life at his full potential. In other words, he wasn't living a purpose filled life because the life he was living was birthed out of his insecurities. He never matured from an egg to a hatchling. He was unfertilized. In other words, he was sterile. He was stuck in the process. Therefore, he compensated for his lack with things, yes carnal things that brought him no real pleasure. He had the accolades of man, but he wasn't happy. He was full of pride and looked down upon others and saw them as less than. To the average onlooker or passerby, he was seen as a distinguished and an important person but the wall that he had built hid his real pain and issues. The wall was built of the best materials and strongest stones and he took confidence that his wall could withstand anything that came his way. The wall signified his own strength, and we know what *Zechariah 4:6 says, "Not by might, nor by power, but by my spirit saith the Lord of hosts."*

He sat on this wall to appear that he was approachable but not really and so that everyone would know him, his power, position and to be seen by men. The wall represented strength, but Humpty Dumpty was weak and fragile. I remember years ago, I was getting ready for church, and I had on what I called my preaching suit. I heard clear as day, "Let me heal you," and I remember screaming, "Noooo!" I told the Lord, "Not now Lord," because the ministry was at a pivotal point, and I couldn't be out of place. The Lord told me, "Let me heal you where you're at now. Or when you get higher in me, I will have to bring you down to heal you." The one-year consecration unto the Lord was the catalyst to jump starting the healing process in my life. He removed the walls, barriers of my mind, psyche, and rebooted my mind and personality. In exchange, I have wholeness of my mind and personality. Just like I had my day of reckoning with the Lord. Humpty Dumpty was warned to deal with the problems of the heart, mind, and soul (Proverbs 16:18). He chose to keep up false pretenses. He didn't want to appear weak and was concerned about what men thought of him. Man is weak without God in our lives, case in point.

One day, Humpty lost his bearings, and footing, and he fell hard. He impacted the ground with a loud thump that everyone heard and saw him fall. His shell shattered in so many pieces and all his insides spilled out onto the ground. The birds began to pick and eat his inwards. Whereas they were unable to put him back together because he was like a puzzle with missing pieces. Humpty Dumpty had the best king's men, the A-Team of specialists, and they couldn't put him back together again. When God created man in His image and likeness, man was an empty shell. Once God breathed the breath of life into us, we became living souls. Humpty Dumpty had it all but what does it profit a man if he shall gain the entire world and lose his soul? His heart and treasure were in the wrong place. He loved the corruptible but it's the incorruptible that matters, Christ Jesus. Humpty Humpty Dumpty was never restored, and he died in a way he feared the most. He was vulnerable and off his wall of false facades. The world's system had a hold on him, and he became like the world. The world was his standard. Appearances were his everything. Position, power, prestige, drugs, alcohol, and relationships will not fulfill you. Humpty Dumpty never transitioned past being an egg. He never matured but he was frozen in time. Biblically walls symbolize hope, protection, strength, and glory. It also means divisions, strongholds, and imprisonment. Walls may be things we need removed from our lives. Everything behind the wall isn't easily seen but is hidden from those that don't need to know. Humpty Dumpty sat on a wall of:

1. Self-importance
2. Authority and strength
3. High Position
4. Seen and esteemed of and by men
5. He was about keeping up appearances
6. Wanted to display strength

Humpty Dumpty was a flawed egg with many secrets behind the wall. There were hidden things not easily seen. He was a prisoner of false facades. He was lonely, insecure, fearful, weak in personality and once again very fragile. One day Humpty experienced a great blow to his wall! Life happened and he lacked the resilience and staying power because his hope and foundation weren't built in God.

Have you ever felt life was so hard and you couldn't take it anymore? 2 Corinthians 12:8-10 tells us when we're at our weakest, God is at His strongest. I know this to be true in my life, having had a mental breakdown while enlisted in the Navy. It was the Lord that kept me when I could feel my mind leave me. Oh, only if Humpty Dumpty allowed God to heal him and had he humbled himself under the mighty hand of God, his story would have ended on a happier note, of Restoration. *Jeremiah 30:17 says, "For I will restore health unto thee, I will heal thee of thy wounds, saith the Lord."*

REFLECTIONS:

1. An admirable trait of Humpty Dumpty was that he was a risk taker. He was an egg and yet he sat high on a wall. It's easier to break an egg than it is to unbreak an egg. In Christ, we must have faith and without it, it's impossible to please God. Throughout the Bible, you'll see countless people told to step out and leave to go to an unknown place or to do this or that. Many of us are waiting and believing for promises and dreams to be fulfilled. Sometimes the promises become a vision that we look at that encourages us to run on and to take a leap of faith. — Hebrews 11:1, Hebrews 11:6, James 2:14-16, Hebrews 10:24.

2. It's so easy to put trust in things and we often do it without thinking. Yet when we need to trust in God. Our flesh and mind will immediately give you reasons why you can't trust God. Humpty Dumpty sat on a wall that was big and strong. He felt protected and confident that the wall

was going to do what it was created to do. His confidence and peace were in a thing that could be destroyed rather than the Great I Am, who is all powerful. The very wall that was sat upon for protection and honor was the thing that caused his demise. — Psalms 146:3, Psalms 20:7, Jeremiah 17:7-8, Isaiah 26:3.

3. Humpty Dumpty hid behind the wall. It kept people at a distance. He was visible before the people, but he was not accessible. God created us as relational beings. Establishing and maintaining relationships is good. Humpty Dumpty had vertical relationships with people that were empty and one sided. I give you absolutely nothing, but you give me your applauses, and your admiration of me. The perfect example of a friend is when Christ gave His life for you and I. — John 15:13, Proverbs 18:24, Proverbs 17:17, and Proverbs 27:9.

4. Humpty Dumpty became complacent and settled by accepting that a wall was all that mattered: to be a well-dressed and prestigious egg that was seen by man and to be highly esteemed. He never reached his full future in life. He never transitioned from being an egg to a hatchling, to know his purpose and to live an abundant life. — Colossians 1:16, Ecclesiastes 3:1, Jeremiah 32:19, Proverbs 19:21, and John 10:10.

5. Keeping up appearances and what people thought of him was important. He was an attention seeker and would get it by any means necessary. The wall was just an illusion, a mirage because behind the wall was a very broken and insecure egg. — Isaiah 26:3, Luke 12:4, Psalms 56:4, Romans 8:8, and Galatians 1:10.

6. Humpty Dumpty, a classy man, was proudful and looked down upon people. He forgot to give God the Glory and be thankful for all the blessings he received in life. When God elevates us, it's so important to remember the Blesser and to stay humble. — Proverbs 16:18, 1 John 2:16, Galatians 6:7, and John 17:16.

CHAPTER TWELVE

Searching The Old Lady in the Shoe

"And above all things have fervent charity among yourselves: for charity shall cover the multitude of sins." — 1 Peter 4:8

"The Old Lady who Lived in a Shoe," is a nursery rhyme written by Mother Goose. There was an old lady that lived in a shoe with her twelve children. She fed them soup without bread, and they went to bed. Not knowing the back story, it would be easy for a person to make assumptions and have opinions. I hear people saying, "Where is her husband? Do all the kids have the same father? Girl, I heard he left for bread and never came back." Before delving in, let me discuss some of the spiritual symbolism first. The Old Lady represents suffering. She experienced and suffered many things and is seasoned with life experiences.

"Many are the affliction of the righteous, but the Lord delivers them out of them all (Psalms 34:19)." Shoe means poverty, depravity, or journey. Bread means substance, provision, the Bread of Life and The Living Word. The Old Lady's current situation wasn't always like this. She once lived in a lovely home in a nice neighborhood with her children and husband. Yes, that's right. She's married, and he provided well for his family. The Old Lady often yearned how they ate bread and meat but now scarcely had enough to eat from day to day. One day her husband left to get some bread and he never returned. I grew up hearing how men would leave to buy a pack of cigarettes, milk, or bread and they were never seen again. They often abandoned their families because the financial burden was too much, or they were simply dead beats.

The Old lady was the talk of the town and if people didn't know the truth, they made stuff up. Can you imagine the heartache, shame, and ridicule she suffered? Not knowing what happened and not knowing if the rumor mill was true. Her and her children had to leave their home and go live in a forest, finding the shoe of a giant and making it their home. She was in limbo and a widow. She was separated or abandoned by a man that said he loved her. Some of the women were just mean, nasty, and they gossiped that she must of ran him off. I relate to her in several ways. I was married at the prime of my life and my husband at the time didn't want to be married anymore. He asked me to give him two years and he'll come back. In the meantime, he slept with so many women and made children within the marriage. I thought I was being the good Christian wife. I prayed and prayed. He knew I took my vows seriously and would never sleep with someone else. In the end, we divorced and I remained single for 20 years. Rumor has it that her husband was captured by a giant and killed. Sometimes she would be seen conversating with an old man that played nick, knack, patty, whack, give a dog a bone. She was given a dirty look and they talked about her kids and his dog. But secretly, she was looking for a father for her kids and she needed financial help.

I used to cry when I first got divorced and I would tell God I needed a husband to pay my bills, to put gas in my car and anything else that I wasn't used to doing. I remember I had a friend that lived in the projects, and I saw such poverty that I had never experienced. Back in the day, the government gave you money according to the number of kids you had. My friend's mother got pregnant because my friend and her brother both graduated high school the same year. You could sense the fear her mom had, that her welfare checks were about to come to an end. Once she got pregnant, I discerned the fear lifting off the whole household. This was the mindset and often, it was generational. Stay pregnant to keep the checks and food stamps coming. At the beginning of the month, the fridge was full, and all the baby daddies would be booed up and when the money was gone, they were ghost.

John 7:24 says, "Judge not according to the appearance, but judge righteous judgement." Making assumptions is toxic and quite dangerous. It does much harm to one being falsely judged and you look like an ass. Cliché: when you assume you make an ass out of you and me. In this context, ass is referring to the four-legged animal that Jesus rode on in the Bible. John 8:1-11 tells the story of Jesus in Mount Olives and in early in the morning, He entered the temple again and the people came to Him, and He taught them. The Scribes and Pharisees bring a woman caught in adultery and they placed her amid everyone. They claimed that she was caught in the very act of committing adultery and according to Moses, she should be stoned. They asked Jesus, "What do you think?" They were trying to entrap Jesus so that they may accuse Him. The Scribes and Pharisees used the woman as a pawn and had no desire in seeing justice being served. If it were true, they would have brought forth the man as well. Both guilty parties were to be stoned according to the Mosaic Law. Jesus knew the intents of their hearts and He didn't say anything. Instead, He began to write on the ground as if He didn't hear them speaking. After a while, Jesus lifted his head up and said, "He that is without sin among you, let him first cast a stone at her." Jesus scooted down and began to write on the ground again. One by one, starting with the eldest, they began to leave, for they were convicted. Jesus was the only one left in her presence and he asked her, "Woman where are those thine accusers? Hath no man condemned thee?" She said, "No man, Lord." Jesus said unto her, "Neither do I condemn thee: go, and sin no more." This passage is a beautiful display of Christ's love.

We see at the beginning of this verse Jesus just left Mount Olives. A place He frequented several times and is symbolic of reconciliation, cleansing, healing, victory, and peace. The scribes and the Pharisees knew that Jesus had disregarded teachings, the Law to heal and bring deliverance. Jesus loves people and souls and he ministered compassion vice condemnation. When he told her he didn't condemn her, we see grace and forgiveness and then he tells her to sin no more. She's instructed to live a Holy life. The religious sector was more concerned with being right and to prove a point. In John 4:4-26, Jesus is weary and sits near a well and it's noon. It's the hottest part of the day because that's when the ray of the sun is at its strongest and hottest. A Samaritan woman comes to pitch water from the well and she sees a man. Jesus asks her for a drink. She is a little astonished because first of all no one is usually here. Secondly, why would this man be speaking to her, a woman? And thirdly, she's a Samaritan and the Jews have nothing to do with them. Jesus began to tell her, "If thou knewest the gift of God, and who it is that saith to thee, Give me to drink; thou wouldest have asked of him, and would give thee living water." Jesus tells her that whoever drinks of this water will never thirst again and that it will spring up like a well of everlasting life. The woman asked Jesus for this water, and He told her to go and bring her husband. The woman tells Jesus I have no husband and Jesus then tells her, yes that's true and you had five husbands and you're shacking up with a man now.

Jesus spoke a word of knowledge that spoke to her present situation. She wasn't accepted by her own people and went out of her way to avoid them. They judged her past and looked down on her because she lived with a man she wasn't married to. Can you imagine what a double blow that had to be to her self-esteem and the rejection she experienced from within her community? Samaria should have been a safe place but it wasn't the case. We see once again how Jesus restores, loves and comfort and ministered right where she was. Love is patient and kind. It doesn't condemn but it restores. When the woman doubted that she'll be able to worship with the Jews, Jesus tells her that it's a heart thing. To worship God will no longer be bound to a certain location by a certain group of people. A day is coming when true worshippers will worship Him in spirit and in truth. In the end, the Samaritan woman was restored, and she ran and told everyone about a man that told her everything about her life. Jesus revealed Himself to her and she believed it to be true. She met the Savior, and her life was never the same, *"Thou wilt shew me the path of life: in thy presence is fullness of joy; at thy right hand there are pleasure for evermore (Psalms 16:11)."* All three women experienced judgement, shame, losses, brokenness, looking for love in all the wrong places and trying to fill a void within them. I didn't grow up in church, yet I had a strong moral compass. I knew it was wrong to be with married men and I never messed with men in relationships. I had an aunt who had a child with a married man. She would often tell me, "Don't mess with a married man because it's a lonely life," and I could hear the pain in her voice. Her pain was because in the end, he chose his family over her. This put a stronger conviction to never go down that lane. Wow! There is so much to say, and I believe it will be for a future book.

REFLECTIONS:

1. I can attest, never judge a book by the cover and never make false assumptions. There is always a back story: the who, what, when, and the how. The old lady didn't always live in a shoe, nor was she financially destitute. There is only one judge, and He is just in all His ways. — Luke 6:37, Matthew 7:1-5, James 4:12 and Romans 14:13.

2. Some sins are visible, and some are hidden. Nevertheless, sin is sin and God knows it is there. Not one of us is perfect but all have sinned and come short of His glory. When Jesus wrote in the dirt the sins of their hearts, they all left because they were convicted. Jesus didn't shout out their sins. He could of if He wanted to. That's the difference between Him and the accusers. He was moved by love, and they were moved by the pride of their flesh. Love restores, gives grace, and forgives. — 1 Corinthians 13:4-8, 1 Corinthians 13:13, Romans 3:23, and 1 John 4:7.

3. The grace of God is more than salvation, but it is everything we need to live a Godly life. It is a gift of God that we are forgiven, our minds are transformed, and our hearts are changed. We see in each case He ministered Grace and they were forgiven, set free and enabled to sin no more and live Holy. They were given salvation for their thirst they were trying to quench through unprofitable relationships. — 1 Corinthians 2:9, Ephesians 2:8-9, Isaiah 55:1-2, Romans 3:24, and Titus 2:11.

4. Not Guilty! You're Forgiven! When Jesus wrote in the sand, it represents that it's not permanent. Your sins can be forgiven. Wiping the dirt is symbolic of our sins being wiped clean. — 1 John 1:9, Isaiah 1:18, Isaiah 43:25, Hebrews 8:12, and Micah 7:9-10.

5. Just one encounter with God can change your life for a lifetime. It is impossible to be in His presence and remain the same. The woman caught in adultery kept her face to the ground and she knew every time she slept with that man, her life was at risk. Yet she continued in a toxic entanglement. Something was broken in her that she didn't

care for her life. I have done things in my life that I never thought I would do. But pain and brokenness will make you hate yourself so much that you'll want to be dead. The woman with five husbands, not only was there something broken but missing pieces and things were out of place in her life. She had a deep hole that she tried to fill with empty wells or relationships. She was even now shacking up with a man because someone told her, "It's better to have a man than be lonely, or I rather have a piece of a man than no man at all." She was afraid to be by herself. People judged her that's why she went all out of the way to get water at the worst time. But Jesus told her whole life story. She was given that water that quenched her thirst, and she was forgiven by grace and set free. Where would you and I be today without God's grace and mercy? I know somewhere dead spiritually and on our way to hell.

CHAPTER THIRTEEN

Oh, It's Going Down- London Bridges.

"For the weapons of our warfare are not carnal, but mighty through God to the pulling down of strongholds; Casting down imaginations, and every high thing that exalteth itself against the knowledge of God and bringing into captivity every thought to the obedience of Christ."
— 2 Corinthians 10:4-5

London Bridges is a nursery rhyme and a sing along song and its author is unknown. As a child, the neighborhood kids and I would line up to play this game. While singing London Bridges, two people would hold their hands up like an arch. Everyone had to run through quickly while we all sang and if the arch fell on you, we would rock that person back and forth and sing, "Take the key and lock her up, my fair Lady." The person was eliminated, and we'll start the game all over again. This is the very rhyme/song that the Lord used to inspire me in authoring this book. I noticed that there is always a dark meaning and back story about how each nursery rhyme, fable, and fairytale came into existence. The London bridge has endured fires, attacks, wears, and tears but it has never fallen. The original bridge was taken down brick by brick because it was cheaper to build a new bridge than to renovate it. The old London Bridge was bought and reassembled in Arizona in the 20th century.

An immurement is a form of punishment and a form of sacrifice. A person would be encased into a room or a wall without an entrance, or exit and left to die. The lyrics, "take the key and lock it her up" are a homage to an inhumane practice and many believe children may have been used as sacrifices.[11] The lyric "my fair lady," is when the bridge was being attacked but it didn't fall because it occurred on the virgin Mary's birthday and the bridge was protected by her. Another explanation is a noble family claims that a descendent was buried in the mooring of the bridge as a form of sacrifice.

In my travels, I've seen and driven on all kinds of bridges. There's a bridge in California and Washington state, that when it rains sometimes the bridges would flood and had to be closed. A bridge is a structure that provides passage over a road or river.

11. All That's Interesting. 2022. Immurement: The Horrifying Fate Of Being Entombed Alive. [online] Available at: <https://allthatsinteresting.com/immurement-history> [Accessed 24 May 2022].

The synonyms for bridges are go over, pass over, crossover, and overpass. To be a bridge for someone is to establish a relation and we know that Jesus is a bridge over troubled waters. He stands in the gap and becomes an overpass over troubled waters. *1 Corinthians 3:11, "For other foundation can no man lay than that is laid, which is Jesus Christ."*

The design of a bridge is critical and must be strong enough to bear its own weight, withstand forces that act on bridges, such as the wear and tear from the weather elements and age stress. Often in times of war, the greatest way to defeat your enemy is to destroy the roadways, giving it the ability to get supplies. In Joshua 6:2, God tells Jericho, *"And the Lord said unto Joshua, See I have given into thy hand Jericho, and the King thereof, and the mighty men of valor."* Before I go further, I want to explain the walls of Jericho and the significance of destroying it. God promised the Israelites a land flowing with milk and honey. There were people that served other gods and were full of sin living in the destined land. God wanted them to rid the people and all their evil attachments so that His people wouldn't become contaminated. Jericho was one of the first permanent communities because, prior to that, we were hunters and gatherers. Jericho was strategically built and was a weapon itself. Its wall was thirteen feet thick, and its tower was twenty-eight feet high, and its walls were built with the strongest materials. The walls protected its inhabitants from outside intruders and its water supply. Jericho was open during the day, but at night, it was closed. Many tried to defeat them but failed and Jericho was a stronghold that needed to be dealt with. A stronghold is a place that's been fortified to protect against attack. It is also a defensive structure or an inaccessible place like a cliff. Lastly, it's a citadel or fortress. To keep and hold are other words for stronghold.

A spiritual stronghold is anything that has a hold on you. Its sin and bondage. Some strongholds are kept secret due to shame and fear. The enemy thrives off this and keeping many in bondage. Below is a list of some strongholds:[12]

1. Bitterness/Unforgiveness
2. Worry/Fear
3. Jealousy
4. Addictions
5. Lust, adultery, meaningless intimate encounters
6. Selfishness/ Fragile Ego
7. Complaining Attitude/Low Confidence
8. Lying/Gossiping/Judgmental/Controlling

Spiritual strongholds must be fought in the spirit and in Joshua 6:1-21, God gave Joshua detailed instructions as to how to defeat Jericho. Ninety nine percent of the battle for a child of God is in the mind. Early in my walk in Christ, I had so many giants and strongholds of my mind that had been there a long time. Like Jericho it had taken up residence in my life and planned to stay permanently. It would take reading the Word of God, prayer, and fasting. *"The Battle Ground of the Mind"* by Joyce Meyers was a life changing book because it taught me how to fight and take every thought contrary to Christ captive.

12. Grace for Single Parents. 2022. What You Need to Know About Spiritual Strongholds. [online] Available at: <https://www.graceforsingleparents.com/spiritual-strongholds/> [Accessed 24 May 2022].

God had them march around Jericho once for six days and six is symbolic of the flesh and their flesh was crucified. On the seventh day, they marched around seven times. The trumpets were blown and when instructed, the people shouted and the walls of Jericho fell flat. WOW! Did you know that Jericho had skilled archers that could shoot at a strand of hair and never miss the mark? The children of Israel marching around the walls of Jericho put them in a vulnerable position, but they believed and obeyed God. The ark of the covenant was usually not taken into battle. God wanted His people to know their enemy and that He was with them. This passage demonstrates that strongholds must be fought in the spirit. *"For though we walk in the flesh, we do not war after the flesh (Ephesians 6:3)."* I learned how to fight and defeat the strongholds of my mind. Any thought that was contrary to God's Word, I immediately rebuked it. I didn't come into agreement with the lie. I instead would quote a scripture that canceled the lie and I agreed with it quickly. Over time, I developed a disciplined mind in Christ and my mind was transformed. *Romans 12:2 says, "And be not conformed to this world: but be ye transformed by the renewing of your mind, that ye may prove what is that good, and acceptable, and perfect, will of God."* The defeat of Jericho was twofold. A powerful enemy was defeated and the Israelites' minds were renewed. They saw that all things are possible in God and that He is a refuge in times of trouble (Psalms 9:9).

I remember in 1987, I saw on the news that President Ronald Reagan told Mr. Gorbachev, a General Secretary of the Communist Party of the Soviet Union to "Tear down this wall." A speech spoken in west Berlin, Germany, was a historical account because the wall was symbolic of communism. In 1989 the wall of Berlin fell, thus marking the end of the communist regime. The news showed people crying and holding crosses. A wall for decades separated the west from the east and families that were separated were united. That wall was a constant reminder of living in bondage, but they were made free, and their lives were restored. There are steps to being delivered from strongholds.

1. Acknowledge the spiritual strongholds in your life. — 1 John 1:9-10
2. Confess the strongholds to God. — Psalms 32:5
3. Pray to God by renouncing the sins that invited in the stronghold. — Proverbs 28:13.

REFLECTIONS:

1. London Bridges itself endured a lot of things but it remained firm in place. This is symbolic that as Christians, we will suffer many things but in God, we will persevere and not be destroyed. — Philippians 4:13, Psalms 34:19, 1 Corinthians 4:8-9, and Psalms 119:71.
2. Nothing or no one is greater than God. What is impossible with man is yet possible in God. He is stronger than any wall in your life. London Bridges and Jericho were viewed as indestructible strongholds, and both had a day of defeat. The Lord is strong and mighty in battle. He is Elohim, the God of creation, and the God of the covenant.— Psalms 24:8, John 1:1, Luke 18:27, and Isaiah 49:8, Matthew 19:26.

3. The children of Israel were given implicit and meticulous instructions and their complete obedience meant victory or defeat. We must be obedient even when it doesn't make sense and in the end, our faith is increased. — 1 Samuel 15:22, John 14:15, Jeremiah 7:21-23, and Romans 5:19.

4. Everything God does is intentional and has a purpose. If we have faith, our purpose will be revealed. On the seventh day, the children of Israel marched around Jericho seven times, and after the priests blew a long blow on their trumpet, only then were they able to shout as instructed, and the wall of Jericho fell flat. To fall flat means God destroyed its very foundation. It was complete. It was done. Once again, six means the flesh or the evil of man. The men of valor were men skilled in battle and intercession. The ark was the presence of God, and the trumpets means victory and celebration. A detailed strategy was given that taught them how to defeat an enemy, a strong enemy. If we listen, God will speak and reveal how to war and battle our enemies. If we listen and obey, we will have the victory. — Psalms 144:1, Isaiah 1:19, Romans 8:31, and Romans 8:37.

CHAPTER FOURTEEN

You Can't Stop Destiny- Cinderella

"For his anger endureth but a moment; in his favor is life: weeping may endure for a night, but joy cometh in the morning." — Psalms 30:5

"Cinderella," a fairy tale written by Charles Perrault, is a childhood favorite of so many girls. There are many versions of this story in movies and book formats.

Cinderella lived a hard luck life. She was an orphan at an early age after the death of her mother in childbirth and later her father. Her father was a distinguished gentleman, a Lord or Baron. He was lonely and wanted a mother for his daughter. He married a widow with two daughters. One day her father left for a trip and never returned and unbeknown to her, he was murdered by her envious stepmother. Technically after her father's death, she was to receive an inheritance, but it was taken by her stepmother. The day a child of God is born, the enemy seeks to stop destiny and purpose. For example, King Herod and Pharaoh decreed that the first-born male son be killed: to stop prophecy and destiny. Cinderella became a prisoner in her own home and lived a limited life and her movements were restricted. She became the houseslave and was made responsible for all the household duties. Cinderella was seen and not seen and was often dismissed by her stepmother and her stepsisters.

As a child I recall when children were told, "You're to be seen and not heard." In other words, your input has no weight due to immaturity and lack of life experience. Everyone needs to feel significant and to be dismissive of anyone doesn't feel good. I believe the elders meant a child should stay in a child's place. Cinderella was hated for no reason. She was mistreated because of her close relationship with her father, for her goodness, her beauty and because of who she was. She is of nobility with the title of Lady, Your Grace and The Honorable. Cinderella's appearance was rugged, unkept, and torn with worn clothes. Her hands were rough from the hard labor. Her feet were calloused and flat. They had no arches because she had no support system. She had no shoes, and her hair was not done. Her stepsisters took and wore her nice clothes and jewelry. They even kicked her out of her own chamber. She would alter her own clothes so they could wear them. She tended to the fire, and she would sew and mend by the fireplace. Her face became darkened and ashen, and she smelled like smoke. The sparks from the fire would singe her clothes and she would fetch water from the well. Her work was never done. She worked from sunrise to sunset and often would be awakened out of her sleep to empty their honey buckets. In times past, Cinderella lived in a beautiful kingdom and home. But now, everything is neglected, and the people are oppressed. Her stepmother and stepsisters weren't appreciative of what they had. They were ungrateful and felt entitled. They were incapable of valuing and adding to anything because they only took and took. They were operating in illegitimate authority and power because they took what was rightfully hers. There was no oil on it, so nothing they did flourished. When the righteous rule, the people rejoice and with an evil ruler, the people groan. The stepmother had a hard heart that was full of envy and bitterness. She was widowed and in a destitute state that she hid well. Her marrying a Lord was a lifeline that rescued her and her daughters' fate just in time. From her first encounter with Cinderella, she was jealous of the relationship she had with her father. Have you had someone jealous of you or disliked you for no reason? The answer is that they had heart issues that needed to be addressed. There were so many reasons why they were envious of Cinderella.

1. Cinderella's beauty, goodness, and meekness.
2. Her nobility as a daughter of a Lord or Baron gave her a title, status quo, and an identity.
3. Lived a nice, pampered, and prosperous life.
4. The stepmother wanted her daughters to have what Cinderella had by any means: a pampered life, a father for her daughters and a title.

Her daughters weren't beautiful and lacked the "It Factor." Let us call "it" the anointing. The spirit of jealousy opens the door to the spirit of hatred, anger, bitterness, and murder. Look at Cain and Abel, Esau and Jacob.

The stepmother reduced Cinderella to living in the attic, once again out of sight and mind. They wanted to make her disappear because her very presence was a reminder of who they weren't and will never be. Sometimes people will dismiss, silence, and overlook you because of their own insecurities or jealousy. They thought this would stop destiny, purpose, and the assignment in your life. Jesus and Moses were hidden from destiny killers. Paul and Silas were imprisoned because they were threatened and told to stop talking about Jesus and they praised God despite of, and they were set free. Jeremiah said he was going to keep the word to himself, but it was like fire shut up in his bones. You can't stop destiny. You can delay or hinder it but you can't stop the move of God. The fairy god mother was Cinderella's destiny helper. She dressed her, provided transportation, and gave her glass slippers. This is symbolic in the natural and in the spirit. The godmother had the words in her mouth that released Cinderella into her destiny.

1. **Dressed**- She spoke life to her identity, purpose, and authority.
2. **Transportation**- Provision was provided for everything she needed to fulfill and complete her assignment.
3. **Glass slippers**- Cinderella had no shoes and her feet became calloused and flat because she had no support system. Feet are symbolic of foundation and mobility. Her

foundational power and inheritance were wrongly taken from her. She was restored to her rightful place of power, authority, and position. A glass slipper is unique. One of a kind and tailor made just for her: a perfect fit. High heel means God was elevating her: her position in the kingdom. The see-through glass means a life of transparency and uniqueness.

People can be different based on their talents, qualities, personality, strengths, opinions, gifts, and achievements. The glass slipper also symbolized to Cinderella, "You are a princess, and you belong at that ball. You were created for this; you were created on purpose for this purpose." It doesn't matter what you have been through, experienced, and where you are right now. You are still who I said you are. Your trials, hardships, and losses don't define you or take away the fact, "You're my daughter, and you are a princess." The glass slippers set her in the right direction. The Lord (godmother) ordered her steps. You see, if her father were alive, she would have attended the ball with him. It was preordained for her to meet the prince because yet in her mother's womb, it was ordained who she was to be. Yes, a princess (Jeremiah 1: 5).

Ephesians 1:11 says, "Also we have obtained an inheritance, having been predestined according to His purpose who works all things after the counsel of His will." The glass slipper was designed purposely to only fit Cinderella. People can copy and imitate you but what God has for you is for you. When you're handpicked by God and it's your appointed time, then it's the season for God's manifestation of every word, promise, vision, and dream concerning you. No devil can stop it! Cinderella was carrying a heavy burden and it weighed her down and took a toll on her. She never complained. She just dreamed. But Glory to God, *Isaiah 10:27 says, "And it shall come to pass in that day, that his burden shall be taken away from off thy shoulder, and his yoke from off thy neck, and the yoke shall be destroyed because of the anointing."* Just like the children of Israel who cried out to God for deliverance and at the right time, God did it (Isaiah 60:22).

The stepmother and stepsisters had a deep-rooted hatred for Cinderella that they did everything possible to erase her very existence. Have you ever been called out your name? Have you ever been called everything but a child of God? There are times when someone may pronounce our name wrong or even call us by the wrong name. The person usually apologizes, and we say, "It's okay." But if they continue to do it, honestly speaking, you don't like it because your name is your identification. To call you anything else is like saying you don't matter. Cinderella isn't her real name but she was called that because she was made responsible for tending the fire. She would go and take a rake and gather the cinders, which are small pieces of partly burned coal or wood. Other words for cinder are ash, ashes, embers, and charcoal. Cinders are usually brown or blackish red. Ashes are symbolic of the ruin of something, and their residue is worthless. Cinderella's life was destroyed, or it appeared to be after the death of her father, and she was treated less than the previous servants. She looked like and smelled like what she was going through, and her former life became like a distant memory with each passing day. Her full name is Mary Beth Ella and her father and everyone called her Ella. Ella means light, beautiful,

fairy woman, and feminine. Our names are our prophecy because you become what identifies you. She was known for having
a beautiful spirit and countenance.

In every version of Cinderella, the glass slipper fits her, and
they are married and lived a happy life. The kingdom is restored.
The people rejoice because of the righteous rule. Everything
that was lost and died was restored. Cinderella didn't render
evil for evil towards her stepmother and stepsisters. She understood the 50/20 Principle of life. *Genesis 50:20 says, "But as
for you, ye thought evil against me; but God meant it unto good, to
bring to pass, as it is this day, to save much alive. "* Cinderella risked
her life by attending the ball that was ordained for her to go to
anyway. Her obedience to the words imparted into her from her
destiny helper, then she put it into action. Faith without works
is dead. She met the prince, and everyone attached to her was
restored. She forgave her abusers, and they were married and
lived in the royal court. They had no access to her and weren't
part of her circle. In Ester 4:1-16, Esther was an orphan and
raised by her uncle and was married to the king. She, too like
Cinderella, was created for such a time as now. There was a plot
to kill her people, the Jews, so she had the people fast and pray.
Esther prayed for the favor to go before the king. She knew it
was a significant risk but one worth taking. "If I perish, I perish." God gave her favor with the king and her people's lives
were saved. We know that all things work together for the good
to them that love him (Romans 8:28).

REFECTIONS:

1. Cinderella was a victim of domestic, emotional, verbal, physical, and financial abuse. She never complained but she only dreamed. She had faith that one day her situation would change. Her outlook and perspective was, "What I'm going through right now is for a greater cause." — John 14:1-3, Proverbs 23:7, Colossians 3:2, and Psalms 62:5-6.

2. Betrayal, abuse, and mistreatment are wrong on all levels, but we must give it all to God. He is our judge and vindicator. Only He can right our wrongs. God will restore all that's been lost, taken, and destroyed. Your ugliness will be made beautiful, and your shame will be turned into double honor. — Isaiah 61:3, Ecclesiastes 3:11, 1 Peter3:9, Romans 12:17, and 2 Corinthians 20:15.

3. We see throughout the Bible on several occasions where God would send angelic help. The stepmother and stepsisters placed a heavy burden on Cinderella and although she never complained, it was beginning to take a toll on her. The Father knows just how much we can bear before breaking. Her destiny helper, godmother, was released in her life at a pivotal, critical moment. Cinderella was encouraged, strengthened, and released into her purpose. God always has a ram in the bush. He will always send help and He's never late but right on time. — Deuteronomy 3:16, Joshua 1:9, Psalms 46:1 and Isaiah 41:10.

About The Author

Sandra L. Ross is a minister, teacher, intercessor, worshipper, and poet. She is the author of, *"It's Raining Wisdom: The Golden Nuggets of God"* and *"Healing Waters: Poems that Heal."* Sandra has served in multiple areas in ministry, but her greatest love is for the broken hearted and those bound by pain from their past. Sandra is a true witness of the wonder working power of God in her life. Sandra experienced the ugliness of abuse and all it entails. She lived her life as a victim. But one day, she heard a word, "It's Not in Vain." With this new perspective, her life was never the same. No longer walking in shame, her mourning was turned into dancing, and she was given beauty for ashes. No longer a victim, Sandra was transformed from victim to survivor and to an overcomer because her wounds did not kill her but birthed in her a passion to see people released from the prisons of pain and be made whole.

References

1. Oxford Reference. 2022. parable. [online] Available at: <https://www.oxfordreference.com/view/10.1093/oi/authority.20110803100304891#:~:text=A%20simple%20story%20used%20to,side%20by%20side%2C%20application'.> [Accessed 23 May 2022].

2. Oxford Reference. 2022. allegory. [online] Available at: <https://www.oxfordreference.com/view/10.1093/oi/authority.20110803095403338> [Accessed 23 May 2022].

3. www.dictionary.com. 2022. Definition of allegory | Dictionary.com. [online] Available at: <https://www.dictionary.com/browse/allegory> [Accessed 23 May 2022].

4. Writer's Digest. 2022. Uses of Allegory. [online] Available at: <https://www.writersdigest.com/improve-my-writing/uses-of-allegory#:~:text=An%20allegory%20is%20a%20narrative,The%20Pilgrim's%20Progress%20(1678).> [Accessed 23 May 2022].

5. Merriam-Webster.com Dictionary, s.v. "press," accessed May 23, 2022, https://www.merriam-webster.com/dictionary/press.

6. www.dictionary.com. 2022. Definition of weather | Dictionary.com. [online] Available at: <https://www.dictionary.com/browse/weather> [Accessed 23 May 2022].

7. www.dictionary.com. 2022. Definition of storm | Dictionary.com. [online] Available at: <https://www.dictionary.com/browse/storm> [Accessed 23 May 2022]

8. Merriam-Webster.com Dictionary, s.v. "storm," accessed May 23, 2022, https://www.merriam-webster.com/dictionary/storm.

9. 2022. [online] Available at: <https://www.collinsdictionary.com/us/dictionary/english/rip-van-winkle#:~:text=Rip%20Van%20Winkle%20in%20British,Word%20origin> [Accessed 24 May 2022].

10. Merriam-Webster.com Dictionary, s.v. "egg," accessed May 24, 2022, https://www.merriam-webster.com/dictionary/egg.

11. All That's Interesting. 2022. Immurement: The Horrifying Fate Of Being Entombed Alive. [online] Available at: <https://allthatsinteresting.com/immurement-history> [Accessed 24 May 2022].

12. Grace for Single Parents. 2022. What You Need to Know About Spiritual Strongholds. [online] Available at: <https://www.graceforsingleparents.com/spiritual-strongholds/> [Accessed 24 May 2022].

Index

D

E

www.ingramcontent.com/pod-product-compliance
Lightning Source LLC
Chambersburg PA
CBHW071010120626
46546CB00003B/1023